Beautiful Holland –
Been Half - in-Love with
you for almost 40 years!

# *Just Another Pilgrim on the Train to Wau*

*Chick Lewis' African Vagabonding Tales
(experienced '75, written '99,
expanded 2003, edited 2023)*

all my best –

Chick Lewis
xx

# About the Author –

**Chick Lewis** is likely one of the most widely-traveled guys you've met, having visited 139 of the qualifying "countries and island groups" on the 'Traveler's Century Club' list.

In January 1975, at the age of 24, Chick gave notice to his job as a physicist, sold nearly everything he owned, and headed out from Los Angeles with $5900 of savings to see the world. And see it he did. In the following 41 months of Super-Low-Budget Vagabonding, he used the cheapest local transport, stretched every dollar, and opened himself up to the beauty of the people and cultures – and adventures – surrounding him, as he circumnavigated the globe.

During this 3-and-a-half-year-long journey, Chick roamed through 60 sovereign nations, seeking out numerous remote, exotic, and often ill-advised locations, some of which are only accessible to the very most determined travelers today. In this book, Just Another Pilgrim on the Train to Wau, are the four months of his African experiences. These range from meeting amazingly generous and good-hearted people to dealing with phenomenally nasty scammers, thieves, gunmen, corrupt officials, and ne'er-do-wells.

If we include the continued journey through Asia, Chick survived quite a number of life-threatening experiences, such as a Fatal Auto Accident, Dysentery, Gangrene, Malaria, Hepatitis, and Dengue Fever, very nearly drowning, a serious tribal fight, and a bandit ambush, making Chick probably also the *luckiest* guy you've ever met.

Returning home after vagabonding, Chick was invited to be first employee of 3D Systems, the company which invented 3D printing. He designed and built the prototypes for the world's first commercial 3-D printers, using resin and lasers, and is named as a co-inventor on at least 18 U.S. Patents. Chick retired in 2009 and resumed traveling extensively... so note:

This travelogue, Just Another Pilgrim on the Train to Wau, covers Chick's tales from Africa. A subsequent book will continue where this one leaves off, including Europe, the Middle East, Asia, Oceania and the Far East.

If you would like to contact Chick, he'd love to hear from you.
chick@Superlowbudgetvagabonding.com
ChickLewis@aol.com

# Chick's Credo for Vagabonding

Mental Preparation Before you Go:

1) Firstly, You must Believe Deeply and Sincerely that you are **JUST ANOTHER DOOFUS**, nobody important or special. All of life made much more sense to me after I fully internalized this fact. Makes it much harder to feel that you are persecuted or unlucky in any current circumstance.

2) Convince yourself that you will be Sick Often, so that you won't become discouraged when it happens.

3) For all of the things you plan to take along, convince yourself that you will LOSE THEM ALL, at least Twice, and get comfortable with that idea. Anything irreplaceable and precious to you, leave it at home.

4) Know that the language barrier will never prevent communication IF you can find someone who is willing to TRY to understand you. Gestures and a few words, if enthusiastically listened to, will always suffice.

After the Launch:
In **Chick's Credo for Vagabonding** one:
- Travels to a new place using local transport,
- Stays in the cheapest available lodging,
- Interacts with the local people,
- Learns twenty words of the local language,
- Eats the local foods,
- Samples the local diseases,
- Experiences the local cultural ceremonies,

- Tries out the local intoxicants,
  – then Decides whether to move on, or to stay awhile longer.

**General and Specific Advice:**
Your attitude is especially important. Unsophisticated people's attitude towards you will 'mirror' your attitude towards them. If you are feeling threatened and closed-down and mean, then you will have a lousy response. If you remain open and friendly and engaging, they will treat you in the same fashion.

Always exhibit confidence. Even if you are lost and alone and worried, you CANNOT allow these feelings to show. They will attract human predators like moths to an arc-light. Always pretend that you are comfortable, exactly where you want to be, and that your plans are moving forward.

Leave maximum flexibility for schedule changes and re-routing. As much as possible, avoid committing to future "hard" dates when you must be somewhere or do something.

Pick a backpack narrow enough that while wearing it, you still fit through a bus doorway.

When crossing borders overland, never buy passage across a border, nor cross as part of a group with folks who you do not know extremely well and COMPLETELY trust. Arrive at the border, detach from everyone, cross the border with your belongings, and find transport again on the far side of the border.

Remember the primary rule of overland travel in Africa:

**"The man with the automatic weapon is always right."**

This work is dedicated to Donna Hampton Reeves, my Love, my Rock and my Inspiration, who has rescued me, physically and emotionally, more times than I can easily recall.

Note on the Images -

All of the photographs are mine, but early in the journey, I was a novice photographer, and made serious mistakes. Many of the images, as you will see, are color-faded and/or 'solarized' due to using bad film, bad development, or postponing development much too long. I hope that the reader can enjoy them in spite of their dodgy quality. After these early learning experiences, I used only Kodak Ektachrome and mailed all of my film back to California for development.

–      Chick Lewis

Lewis/Heaton Publications © 2023

# TABLE OF CONTENTS

*Communards*

*Staying Hydrated*

*Curious Bushman*

*First Farangi*

*Primal Man*

*Wild Animals and Wild People*

*Self Congratulation begins a Bit Too Early*

*Six Ampoules*

*Wau as a Tourist Destination*

*Disturbing Foods*

*Mister Bojo*

*By Truck to Juba*

*Green Mangos, mostly*

*Welcome to Juba*

*Dinka Dances*

*The Mean Drunk*

*Chick's Credo of Low-Budget Vagabonding*

*Boarding the Nile Steamer*

*Lake Victoria from the Air*

*Border Crossing Advice*

*Nairobi*

*Gangrene Diagnosis*

*Confidence Men*

*Busted for dope!*

*Photo Safari into the Veldt*

*Ohio State East African Zoological Study*

*Hyena Encounters*

*Olduvai Gorge*

*Stampede*

*Hepatitis Diagnosis*

*Twiga Beach*

*Sea Snakes*
*Lamu Island*
*Unexpected Romance*
*Malaria Diagnosis*
*Cross-Cultural Pollution*
*Ethiopian Hotels*
*Home Brewed Liquer*
*Addis Ababa*
*Central Tourist Office*
*The Shoa*
*Blue Nile Gorge*
*Fly Capital of the World*
*Blue Nile Falls*
*Gondar*
*Black Jews*
*Shifta Ambush!*
*When You Eat, I Eat*
*Long-Lost Ark of the Covenant*
*Legend of Menelik*
*Feast of Saint Michael*
*Pre-Owned Protective Charms*
*Asmara*
*Kagnew Station*
*Local Girlfriends*
*Eritrean Liberation Front Hits the base*
*Job Offer*
*Taxi Shakedown*
*Out of Africa*
*Curious E-mail*
*Fate of the Film*

# Just Another Pilgrim on the Train to Wau

# CHICK LEWIS' AFRICAN VAGABONDING TALES

*(experienced '75, written '99, expanded 2003, edited 2023)*

The dusty train screeched to a halt half an hour after the attack, with every passenger sorting himself out, climbing back up onto the roofs, finding and securing their belongings. During this confusing time my newest Sudanese buddy Mister Adam appeared at my elbow, saying "Men are hurt, Mister Chih-Kuh, and you must come to see them." I wasn't sure what he meant, but accompanied him a few carriages forward to where the casualties were being collected. That was when I discovered that out of 2000 people on the train, my white skin and tiny 1" by 1" by 3" first aid kit made me the best approximation we could find for a doctor!! Well, alright then, I went back to my Boy Scout and Emergency-Room-Orderly training, and began treating the wounded as best I could. How I found myself riding on the roof of a passenger carriage pulled by a steam locomotive across the deserts of Southern Sudan can be understood only if I am permitted to rewind the calendar by a few months.

February was cold in 1975, and I found myself in the tatty little western-Sicilian port town of Trapani waiting for the weekly ferryboat to Tunis in North Africa. I had been "on the road" for only six weeks, hitch-hiking south from Germany through Italy, and heading for warmer climes, planning to hitch-hike eastwards across North Africa from Tunisia through Libya to Egypt, and then travel south up the Nile into Central (much warmer) Africa. There were a few other tourists in Trapani, and quite a number of Sicilians were boarding the big, modern ferry that morning, with the customary rude pushing and shoving that seem to be necessary any time lines form in southern Italy.

# SOUTH ACROSS
# THE MED

Once on board I met a very interesting Chilean vagabond named Antonio, who had boarded earlier in Palermo. Antonio had been "on the road" for two years already, was an experienced low-budget traveler, speaking perfect English, and apparently great Italian and French. He seemed well-centered, and not too crazy, so we chatted most of the 8 hour ride across the Mediterranean headed for a new continent. We were both surprised to learn that the other planned to hitch across Libya to Egypt, as very few vagabonds took that route. Each had heard lots of terrifying stories of crimes and violence against vagabonds in North Africa, and each happily told the other every one of the tales of muggings, unprovoked weapon attacks, strong-arm robberies, and casual murders.

# TUNISIAN TROUBLES

Dark had already fallen when we entered the harbor of Tunis, though it was not too late at night. The thousand or so Sicilians and Tunisians on board had been jammed up at the loading door on the port side for hours before we sighted land. That whole side of the ship was a huge scrum of people and luggage jammed together uncomfortably overfilling the passageways. I had a flash of intuition. I went to the starboard side of the ship and stood against the deserted mirror-image door in that passageway. Antonio did the same. We had nothing to lose. Ten minutes later, when it became clear to the masses of local passengers that the ship was approaching the pier on the starboard side, a huge rush of obnoxious people came slamming around the corners from both directions and pinned us against the exit doors themselves !! As a result, I was the very first passenger to clear the slow and inefficient customs area into North Africa, and Antonio was the second.

We exited into the darkness, and found ourselves alone on a high pier 60 feet above the water, with 200 feet of long dark sloping ramp, handrails on both sides, leading down straight ahead into the darkness of the port area. It was very still and quiet, no air moving, and only the sound of the water lapping far below. Not a very welcoming scene. As we started side by side down the narrow, deserted gangway, four shadowy shapes detached themselves from the darkness on either side, and silently began to follow us at a distance of only 20 feet ! My neck swiveled around trying to get a look at the men behind us while also searching for more threats somewhere in the darkness ahead.

Antonio, who was similarly disturbed, said "That was quick !" meaning that we hadn't even actually set foot on North Africa yet, and already the situation was deteriorating. About that time I realized a strange thing. The two pairs of threatening shapes silently following us had fallen into perfect step, and now seemed to be MARCHING along behind us !! Before we could even try to figure out what that might mean, they broke into a rousing chorus - "Une kilometre a piedi, a piedi, a piedi ! Une kilometre a piedi - " which I recognized as a French scouting song!! Soon we both joined in the raucous singing, marching triumphantly down the gangway with our escort of Tunisian Boy-Scouts!! After that fine learning experience I never again jumped to bad conclusions, and paid little heed to the horror stories of North African violence.

At the exit gate from the docks area, taxis were waiting, and tourist passengers were in great demand, because they could be cheated more easily, plus the drivers could get kickbacks by delivering them to specific hotels. Antonio and I did some bargaining, and my schoolboy French revealed itself to be very useful. Almost every adult in Tunisia spoke French, and spoke a particularly clear, simple, idiom-free version of the language, making the Tunisians easier to communicate with than the Italians had been, and easier than Parisians later proved to be. We arranged for a small dilapidated cab to take us into the "far side of the Casbah" in the center of town where the cheapest lodging was to be found. Just as we were pulling away we spotted a Canadian couple exiting from the docks, and loaded them, too, into our taxi, much to the disappointment of the other cab drivers.

## Souk of Tunis

Before too long we were checked-in to small, grotty, upstairs rooms in a crumbling building halfway up the hill to the Citadel in Old Tunis proper. By then it was about nine at night, but we four low-budget tourists sallied out into the souk for some food. It was a fascinating place, especially since Tunisia was the first Muslim country any of us had ever visited. By peeking through doorways, we saw lots of interesting things -- craftsmen plying their trades, women wearing the traditional complete body-covering robes and veils, blue tattoos on chins and lips of some women proclaiming their Berber heritage. We met an old guy who told us vehemently in German that the Americans and the Brits and the French were all worthless toadies, and the best people in the world were the Germans. He was quite insulting, and we finally got him to tell us about working for the Germans when they fought in North Africa in 1941/42. We found a cheap eatery, and I introduced myself to "brique a l'oeuf", a wonderful dish. Pastry is wrapped around a raw egg, and a little cheese, and the whole thing is fried up. I ate quite a few brique a l'ouef and enjoyed them hugely.

## Human Shield

While we were wandering around in the confusing dark narrow streets, a big commotion with lots of shouting began. We four foreigners were standing in the recessed doorway of a shop when a man with a knife in his hand came running up at full speed, screaming incoherent words. He grabbed the Canadian husband from behind with an arm around his throat, spun him around, still screaming, and began slashing frantically at the air in front of him and his unwilling shield. Then I spotted the object of his fear. Another Tunisian with a knife held at his side approached, walking slowly and determinedly. I had never before witnessed Death gazing out of a pair of eyes. This slowly approaching Tunisian tough was DANGEROUS, and the squalling prey trying to hide behind his Canadian human-shield knew it! I was SO surprised, that, embarrassingly, I did nothing. For years I had trained myself to DO SOMETHING whenever a situation goes to Hades, and violence breaks out. Usually I take immediate action, and about half the time I do the right thing, and half I do something wildly inappropriate. But this time I just stood there with my mouth open! Very fortunately, the situation resolved itself without my intervention. The Canadian guy freed himself from the terrified embrace of the chased local, who babbled apologetic, incoherent Arabic at the glowering, threatening opponent. Other people who apparently knew both men arrived, inserted themselves between the knife-armed pair, and after considerable argument, turned the pursuer away from his quarry. We were glad about that. The following morning we found out from the locals that the part of the souk we had been wandering through in the middle of the night was the area which is considered so dangerous that the gendarmes don't patrol there after dark.

First sunrise in Africa found me headed for the ruins of ancient Carthage. Those familiar with ancient history will remember that the Romans "left not one stone upon another", and plowed salt into the fields when they finally conquered rival Carthage. Seems that must be literally what happened, because there are NO above-ground remains to be seen. The existing excavated structures are the sewer systems, and the fancy vaulted steam heating tunnels from below the Carthaginian public baths.

Subterranean Ruins of Carthage

But there are also the ancient cemeteries. One called the "Tophet" in particular chilled my soul. The principal deity of the Carthaginian culture was Baal, a bloodthirsty god who demanded the sacrifice of each couple's firstborn child as an offering. And the Carthaginians really did sacrifice thousands and thousands of their infants, burning the tiny corpses and putting the remains in little clay pots which were then buried in ground sanctified to Baal. The display area at the Tophet had EIGHT LAYERS DEEP little tiny pots, over thousands of square feet !! The remains of tens of thousands of sacrificed babies were there, stacked one upon another. The latest burials showed that the Carthaginians had gotten a little less religiously pure. Many of the top layer pots had been found to contain the charred remains of animals, apparently sacrificed in place of the firstborn children.

After three interesting days in and around Tunis, I hitch- hiked easily 60 miles south along the coast to the city of Sousse, and bought a dormitory bed at the youth hostel ("alberge de jeunesse") there. Sousse was comfortable but not too interesting, being mostly a coast resort area for European tourists, and mostly shut down for the winter.

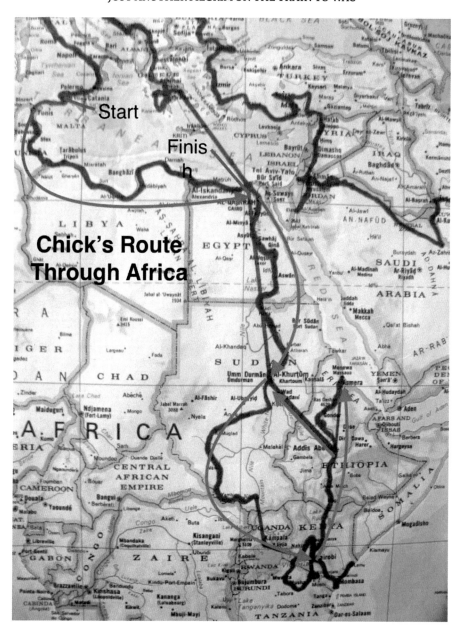

## *Busman's Bluff*

The second morning in Sousse I accompanied some of the folks from the Youth Hostel to the bus station, to send them off to the west, their ultimate destination being Morocco. Buses in Tunisia all had large steel luggage racks on the roof, this being necessary because traveling Tunisians carry heaps of worldly goods with them. Loading the luggage is a time-consuming chore, and it was going on as we arrived at the bus depot. Three Tunisian men were handling the loading, and it was standard practice to tip the loaders for taking care of your personal luggage. Therefore there was one guy handing the luggage up onto the top of the bus, one guy up there packing it in the luggage rack, and one guy standing at the bottom accepting luggage for loading, and collecting the tips. There are plenty of tourist-specific scams in North Africa, all designed to part the tourist from as much of his money as possible. Many of them seem to involve pointlessly hassling a tourist until he simply disgorges money, just to avoid the hassles. Others involve making sure that tourists pay much more for any simple service or product than the locals pay. The little scam we witnessed that morning was a combination of the two.

As the loading was progressing, Martin, one of two Australian vagabonds tipped the Tunisian guy for loading their backpacks. The busman demanded a larger tip from the Australian, although the tip was the same amount he had been accepting from all the locals. Martin ignored him. Then the guy on the top of the bus held the Aussie's backpack out over the side of the bus, threatening to drop it off if the tip were not increased. Martin steadfastly ignored him, too. The loader on top of the bus shouted aggressively at the tourist, and shook his pack out over empty space, threatening again to drop it unless the tip was increased. At this point the lanky, travel-worn, longhaired guy from down under made a rude finger gesture to the loader, who promptly followed through on his threat, and dropped the backpack. It hit the pavement with a nasty noise, breaking welds on the aluminum frame. Dozens of people stopped and watched to see what Martin would do. He didn't look perturbed at all, but walked calmly to the rear of the bus and started climbing the ladder to the roof. Things were getting pretty interesting !! The loader at street level was hollering at him, and tugging at his pant leg to try to deter him from climbing, and the loader up on the luggage rack hollered even louder with threatening-sounding bombast. Our vagabond hero reached the bus roof, and began calmly stepping over luggage in the rack towards the backpedaling loader. Everyone caught their breath as the loader pulled a wicked-looking long folding knife out of his pocket and opened it, holding it in his right hand, while continuing to shout threats and imprecations. The Aussie vagabond never broke stride, continuing to advance casually while bringing a small clasp knife out of his own pocket and opening it, never taking his eyes off of the retreating busman. Just as blood was about to flow, the nerve of the bluffing loader snapped. He scuttled down over the windshield and hood of the bus, hitting the pavement running, promptly disappearing out of sight around a corner. Everyone started to breathe again, whereupon Martin pocketed his knife, and called down to me, "D'ja giv'us a hand here, mayt ?" The three of us proceeded to load all of the other Tunisians' luggage up onto the roof gratis, no more tips were necessary. I'm willing to bet that the bus luggage crew in Sousse never jettisoned another vagabond's pack. Down-under Martin had won the tense confrontation without ever speaking a word or changing his mildly annoyed expression.

When I had explored Sousse sufficiently, I went hitching south towards the Libyan border along the main highway. Hitch-hiking was ok, not wonderful, and I got several short rides with nice, French speaking Tunisians. In the late morning an old, faded Citroen passenger vehicle piloted by an elderly redheaded Parisian-born woman who had lived in Tunisia for almost 30 years pulled over. Driving south we had a good chat, and she explained that she was leaving the main road and driving out to a village on the coast called Mahtma, where she lived. I checked my little road map and found a road coming back from Mahtma to a point farther south on the main road, so I went along. She let me down in wonderful blazing sunshine with a salty sea breeze in front of a strange little carpentry-cum-junk shop. It displayed for sale, cheap, two actual ancient amphorae. You know, the old jars with two curving handles for carrying. They were mostly covered with barnacles, so it seemed that they had probably been netted by the local fishermen, and ended up there. I regretted that they were so heavy, as I would have loved to have purchased them. This find indicated to me that I was probably not on the beaten tourist path there at Mahtma. Inside the shop were a few more relics, a derelict, tinny blunderbuss, a rusty saber with the tip broken off, and a German second-world-war ammunition pouch. Aha! That reminded me of my quest for war relics.

## *War Relics*

Before I left California I had been asked by my younger brother Mark, to search out for him a genuine WWII leather battle harness, from which the German soldiers suspended their gear. Mark had done the research, and informed me that in German it would be called "Wehrmacht Strumpfhalter". Therefore, when I had found myself in southern Germany, I had visited antiquity/ military stores, and faithfully asked the proprietors if they had any Wehrmacht strumpfhalter. The answer was always "Nein", but I thought they were looking at me a little funny. Finally one nice German shop owner, who spoke English, figured out what I really wanted, and took pity on me. The true objects of my search were called "Wehrmacht Hosentrager", which is to say, "suspenders". What I had been asking for were actually "German Army Garter Belts" !!

The carpenter's relic shop was only attended by a little girl of about four years who spoke exclusively Arabic, so I waited there for 45 minutes until the proprietor returned. Nope, no battle harness, but that had been a real long shot anyway.

## Meerab the Tunisian fisherman

As I strolled through the tiny seaside town of Mahtma, I enjoyed the view of the Mediterranean, and chatted with the friendly people, shortly walking out of town to the south. My method for hitch-hiking is to walk in the direction I want to go, turning around to thumb any vehicles when I hear them coming up from behind, and continuing walk quickly backwards while thumbing. Nope, I haven't tripped over things TOO many times while walking backwards that way.

After hiking for 15 minutes without a single vehicle passing, I realized that I had probably made a tactical error in coming to Mahtma. According to my map it was about 40 kilometers back out to the main road, and I resigned myself to "hoofing it" all that way. But it was a beautiful warm day, and my backpack fit well, and my boots were still in good shape, and all in all I was content to be marching along the rim of the sea. I saw a shape on the far side of the road approaching me from the opposite direction. It turned into a Tunisian man and a small six-year-old girl, accompanying a tired- looking donkey with huge clay jars hanging on either side of its saddle. The little procession, when they spotted me, crossed the road to confront me. The gray-robed gentleman assailed my ears with a happy torrent of French. "Ah, you are a tourist !! We LOVE tourists ! My name is Meerab, and I am a fisherman. I have a small boat. Please, please, come to stay with me in my house on the beach, we will eat cous cous, and tomorrow you can go fishing with me !! You are welcome !! Please agree to come and visit !! You will ?? You will ?? Ah, good, here, my daughter will take you to my home and I will speak more with you after I return from fetching water." Going out in a small boat to learn traditional fishing really sounded good to me, and, quite willing to accept Meerab's hospitality, I allowed my index finger to be grasped by Shala, his eldest daughter, who almost ran back with me along the road to the south. After a few minutes she started to call out loudly and excitedly in Arabic, and a dozen other children of both sexes magically appeared, including both of Shala's younger sisters. The whole cavalcade accompanied me to the crest of a low bluff, which revealed a storybook fishing village of a dozen mud-brick houses laid out between the bluff and the clean sand beach, with the blue-grey Mediterranean just beyond. The children were all very excited, and immediately taught me their one game. They called it "Cour, Cour !", which they took to mean "run, run" in French. Yes, that was the game. We would shout "Cour, Cour !" and run madly along the beach together, then repeating the process in the opposite direction. After tiring of their game, I took my frisbee out of the backpack, and taught them to throw it. As you can imagine, this toy immediately supplanted "cour, cour" as the favorite past- time, and pretty soon some of the older children could successfully throw and catch the Frisbee. Invariably, those unfortunate enough to catch the toy were knocked down and piled onto promptly by their fellows. But it was a grand day, and a grand game ! After some time playing, Shala took me home and introduced me to Fatima, her mother, and her baby brother Ayab.

Meerab's nine-foot-short, shabby, peeling wooden dory sat comfortably on the sand near his home. His nets were stretched along the beach drying in the sun. The family home was very small, consisting of one 12 foot by 12 foot room for the 3 sheep, donkey, dog, chickens, and cat, and another very similar room in which lived the humans. There were no windows, no pieces of furniture, and the kitchen consisted of a pump-gas brazier, stored in a niche in the wall when not in use. Fatima was probably a few years younger than my age of 24, but years are not kind to child-brides in Tunisia, and after four children, she looked about 40. She was short, hugely fat, ready to give birth for the fifth time at any second, and had a continual horrible, bubbling, tubercular cough. But she was REALLY glad to meet me, and made me feel extremely welcome !! Fatima didn't speak any French, but she made herself understood quite well in voluble Arabic with gestures, and sat me down inside, storing my backpack in a corner, and showing me a little photo of a young Swedish vagabond named "Christopher" whom she lead me to understand had stayed with them for several weeks some years previously.

Not long after that Meerab returned with the two big jars of water, and sat conversing with me for an hour or so. He was interested in where I came from, and where I was going, and all the usual stuff. He let it be known that we should have a celebration, and I donated some money to the cause, at which point Meerab left again for town, on a shopping trip. I played outside with the village children while he bought coffee, peanuts, condensed milk, tea, cous cous, and a few sheep vertebrae, returning later from Mahtma.

Names changed and faces cartooned to avoid any embarrassment

Tunisian Fishing Family

By that time it was early evening, and while Fatima prepared the cous cous with sheep backbones on the floor in her pressure cooker, Meerab and I sat on the sand, while he smoked and repaired tears in his nets, looping them though his toes for tension as he worked. The children had finally run out of energy, and sat around in a tired circle as the sun set behind us, lighting up the clouds scudding across the ocean to our front with rose hues. The modern world was far away. Except for the cigarette, it was a scene which could have been taken unchanged right out of the Bible.

We enjoyed our evening meal, and small glasses of very strong coffee, by the light of a tiny ceramic oil lamp, just like those found in museum cases worldwide. By this time Meerab was wearing my wrist watch, and Fatima was wearing my magic traveling bangle. The little girls had discovered my hairbrush, with which they had fallen deeply in love, never having been able to brush out their hair before that evening. Combs were not nearly as much fun as the hairbrush.

And then it was time to sleep. The floor of the house was cleared, sheepskins were spread out, baby Ayab was wrapped up and put in his niche in the wall, and the three other children laid out in a row. I got out my sleeping bag, and unzipped it. "Ah," said Meerab, "what a wonderful blanket!" and when I turned around again, I found that the three girls were fast falling asleep under it. Hmmmm, well, okay, I took the children's threadbare blanket and rolled up my jeans in a bundle against the wall to use as a pillow. When I turned around again, there was Meerab, with his head on my jeans, under the children's blanket facing the wall, rapidly falling asleep. Hmmmm, well, that left an open place on the floor between Meerab and Fatima. I stood there for a few uncertain seconds in the dim flickering light of the oil lamp, thinking of how different one culture could be from another, while Fatima offered the space to me. "Keef- keef" she said softly, meaning we are just the same, all brothers and sisters. I lay down in the open zone, whereupon a hundred famished bedbugs and fleas emerged from the old sheepskins and began to bite and tickle me.

I lay there on my back, with Meerab sleeping peacefully just at my right shoulder, and the imposing wall of Fatima's back and buttocks just to my left. All too soon, I sensed the buttocks quietly inching ever closer to me. Fatima half rolled over, and in the dim light of the trimmed-down oil flame, I could see that she was making definite "goo goo eyes" at me. "Leht" (no), I whispered. " - - leht, leht, leht", but soon I was being groped powerfully and intimately by the extremely pregnant woman, meanwhile avoiding massive lip-crushing Tunisian kisses !! It was an AWFUL: situation, because, from what I knew of Muslim customs, if Meerab, sleeping at my elbow, awoke, he would have NO choice except to kill me !! What was I gonna do ?? Well, in horrible interpersonal situations my first solution has always been direct honesty. I grabbed Meerab by his shoulder and shook him. "Meerab, wake up, you've gotta wake up." That was when I discovered that Meerab, bless his duplicitous heart, was only pretending to sleep. He was sporting a dandy hard-on and just waiting for Fatima to get me warmed up !! What my new friends had in mind was apparently a pita bread sandwich with American cheese. Having always been boringly binary, that is NOT what I had planned for the evening !!

This was certainly the strangest situation in which I had ever found myself. My impulse was to depart immediately, but with my things scattered all over the house, this would not be easy. I had a small epiphany, and my schoolboy French did not fail me as I said to my aroused host, "Oh, Meerab, it is against my religion to sleep with another man !". He stopped, believed me, looked disappointed, and replied, "Well, there is my wife !" - -

- "Oh, Meerab, it is also against my religion to sleep with the wife of another man !" Soon poor dejected Meerab and I had changed places, with me now against the wall with my head on my bundle, under the children's blanket. Between suspicion of Meerab and the biting bugs, I got no sleep that night. Sheep came in from the other room twice in the night and had to be ejected. One of the sheep carried the family cat curled up comfortably asleep in a warm nest on its back.

In the morning it was unfortunately too windy to go out fishing. So I retrieved and packed up my stuff, giving my hairbrush to Shala and her sisters, but ignoring all entreaties to leave my Frisbee behind as well. I gave Meerab a small amount of money for the baby which was due so soon, and, when Fatima realized what I intended, she scooped up the existing baby, and happily held him up in front of my face. "Yeah, OK, Fatima, here's a little for Ayab as well." I said my good-byes and the village kids accompanied me for a quarter mile along the road. I marched steadily southward imagining what a lovely stay "Christopher", Meerab's Swedish house-guest, must have had here.

AM hitching proved to be better, and I saw the impressive still-standing ruins of the very intact roman-built coliseum in the town of El Djeb. After passing through the town of Sfax, that evening I reached Gabes, and slept at the youth hostel ("beet shebab") there.

## *Flying Dutchman*

A number of young vagabonds were staying at the youth hostel, including my friend Antonio, and Jerry, a Dutchman, who had apparently been driving back and forth across Northwest Africa in his rattletrap diesel Mercedes for years. A number of us pooled our resources to buy fuel, and a team of our Nederlander pilot, an American, a Chilean, a Canadian, a Swiss, and a Norwegian rode with the "flying Dutchman" inland to see the oasis town of Chenini, as pictured on all of the Tunisian tourist brochures. It was a very spacey experience to ride in the Mercedes, windows up, a/c on, with the Rolling Stones blasting from the tape player, and look out the window to see faceless tattooed women in black robes, holding their white veils in place with their teeth, camels pulling plows through the stony soil, and other disorienting sights. On our way we stopped at a beautifully maintained German war cemetery, in close proximity to two interesting concrete pillbox emplacements built by the Germans in 1942 to command the main road. More than 10% of the German graves were marked "unknown".

All of the fresh vagabonds with the exception of yours truly were extremely excited about the desert scenery away from the coast. They couldn't stop talking about how amazing it was, never having seen a real desert up close before. I kept my mouth shut, as it was really just like the familiar deserts of Western America, where I had done plenty of camping, and therefore the scenery seemed normal to me. In the early afternoon we reached the oasis of Chenini, a strip of vividly green date palm trees surrounded by dun-colored rocks, which was about two miles long, but never more than 200 yards wide. Now THAT was something new and exciting for me to see, and I became as enthusiastic as everyone else!

We stopped the car near some mud-brick buildings and started wandering around. The local people were friendly, and seemed glad to see us. But there were no souvenir shops, and nobody was trying to sell us anything, and that seemed rather strange until we figured out that there are TWO oases called Chenini in Tunisia, and we were at the one without the eight-story-high cliff full of picturesque hollowed-out rock dwellings!

# Our Chenini

The "Chenini" which all the tourist brochures were touting was another 140 kilometers southwest, by a different road from the coast. Oh, well, we all agreed to check out "our" Chenini, well off the tourist path, and see what there was to be seen. Surprisingly, there were quite a few interesting things in that small green desert outpost. When one of the local boys offered to show us the alligators, we snorted in derision, but soon we were having an impromptu tour of a crocodile farm ! We saw the spring where the water just bursts upward out of the sand, and had a drink of the wonderful, cool artesian water. An old French redoubt, said to have been built by the romantic French Foreign Legion, also displayed its ruins to us. And I found some really interesting and colorful bugs and caterpillars, new to my experience.

From Gabes, a few days later, Jerry drove four of us in the pay-as-you-go Mercedes transport south to the resort isle of Djerba, separated from the mainland by a narrow channel of salt-water. There were a few big resort hotels on a long, windy beach, mostly closed down for the season. Nothing of any historical or cultural interest was to be found, so before too many more days had passed, Antonio and I found ourselves standing at dusk at the Tunisian/Libyan border post, planning to hitch-hike across Libya to Egypt together.

## I almost Enter Libya

Clearing the Tunisian outgoing formalities was easy, but I was refused entry by the Libyans. Rats, they told me my one week transit visa had already expired ! I had gotten the visa in Rome more than a month before, and in order to even apply for a visa, I had to pay to have all of my passport information translated into Arabic characters by an approved translator, and then pay to have an approved checker certify it as correct. Once this was accomplished and notarized, I had abandoned my passport at the Libyan consulate after informing them of my plans. It came back stamped with a visa, all in Arabic, of course, giving me one week to cross Libya from Tunisia to Egypt. No tourist visas were possible. The Libyan border officials now informed me that, instead of having a week from the time I entered Libya, my week had started on a particular day, and already expired. Of course they hadn't told me that, and, not being able to read Arabic script, the first time I realized it was as Antonio waved to me from inside Libya, and I turned away back into the dark Tunisian night.

I paid way too much for a share taxi ride to Ben Gardane, the nearest town inside Tunisia, because the cabbie knew I had no other options, and therefore no bargaining power. Once in Ben Gardane I was taken in for the night by a very nice schoolteacher and his brother. Neither of these good men concealed any shady second agenda behind their genuine hospitality. The following morning I hitch- hiked 200 miles back north to Sfax, the site of the nearest Libyan consulate. Libya under Muhammar Khadafi was an interesting place. Having everything in Arabic was such a serious issue, that Khadafi had ordered 1600 concrete kilometer posts along the main coastal road to be uprooted, to be replaced by new posts. The new markers carried only Arabic numerals, while the discarded ones called out the kilometers in both Arabic and roman numbers. But that is getting a bit ahead of the story.

## Port Town of Sfax

Once returned to Sfax, I took a very cheap room with thin walls above a tavern/teashop in the wrong part of town. A large ground-floor area of round tables was surrounded by a second floor interior balustrade, behind which were the rooms. It was very noisy, with perhaps 50 or 60 Tunisian card players using the tables to play a four-handed game with standard decks, and thick with cigarette smoke. Everyone played the same game, and there seemed to be no variation. The dictates of Tunisian manhood required that as each card was played, it be "snapped" down forcefully on the table. The result was a very noisy area, with a continual papery snapping crackle and a loud hum of Arabic conversation. In the morning I searched out the Libyan consulate and applied for a new visa. My passport info was already in Arabic, but still, it would be three days before they could process the paperwork. Well, I settled down to enjoy the place for a couple of days, even though there was NOTHING of real interest to see or do in the harbor town of Sfax.

## Riffle Shuffle

When I returned to my tavern, I sat at an unused table and ordered a glass of tea for myself. Shortly I was engaged in conversation with some of the card players, and soon was initiated into the rules of their one simple card game. My new card-sharp friends were determined that I play, and made a space for me at their table. Gratifyingly, I lost the first few hands we played. Each dealer in turn would place all the cards face down in the center of the table and then stir them around with the palms of his hands to randomize them. When it was my turn to deal, I took the pack, "riffle shuffled" it, and riffle-reassembled the deck. "Brrrrrrrrrrrrraakk -- -- Brrrrrrrrrrrooshh" Immediate dead silence reigned in the always-noisy room with every goggling eye in the place paying rapt attention as I riffle shuffled the cards a second time. With amazement, my new friends told me they had seen this behavior in films, but had never before seen it first-hand ! Ah, an unexpected talent in the vagabond ! I offered to teach them to shuffle the cards that way, and pandemonium ensued. Every one of 50 Tunisian men wanted to learn ! But I limited the hands-on lessons to just the three guys at my table, so that they could gain status. After about half an hour, two of them could riffle haltingly, so that most of the cards didn't fly across the table. They were thrilled !! I never had to buy myself a tea or soda for the remainder of my stay there. Every time I walked through the bar on the way to my upstairs room several men would buy me drinks in the hopes that I would teach them to shuffle like the riverboat gamblers of the movies. Naturally the few Tunisians who learned the trick from me refused to teach it to any of their fellows, and endeavored to discourage me from giving lessons to anyone else !

## Abdul-Jabbar

That afternoon in Sfax I met a student named Abdul-Jabbar, who was 17 years old, and interested in all things American. He was thrilled to learn that the best basketball player in the world shared his name! We got on well together, I was invited to his mother's little apartment for a light dinner, and we buddied around town together the next two days. But even with Abdul-Jabbar's encyclopedic local knowledge, there wasn't anything interesting to do or see in Sfax. Sauntering around by myself the second morning, I saw a gaggle of eight non-Tunisians in white uniforms. They were obviously sailors of about my age, and when they spoke to me in American idiom, I discovered that the U.S. Navy missile cruiser 'Little Rock' had docked in Sfax that morning. My new American sailor friends couldn't speak any French, and wanted to know how to ask "Where is the discotheque?" in that language. I taught them, and they were very pleased to find that the long word in the query is exactly the same in both languages ! They wandered off muttering "ooo aee luh discotheque" to themselves so that they wouldn't forget.

# Excitement with my
# Fellow Countrymen

That night, Abdul-Jabbar and I were traversing the dock area just before midnight, headed back towards my cheap lodging and his apartment. The damp, grotty lanes were almost completely deserted, but we ran into a group of six American sailors headed back from their Cinderella liberty which would expire at midnight. Of the six, four of them were some of the same guys I had befriended with translation earlier in the day, the other two being older, "saltier" swabbies. They were all drunk, and hadn't yet had their fight for the evening. This was a bad situation.

The two older sailors came up to me on the echoing dark street, and couldn't help but notice my straight, shoulder-length hair and jewelry. They decided to deride me for being, in their eyes, a homosexual, making lots of rude, mincing comments about how beautiful they found me, including the details of the sexual acts they intended to enjoy with such a pretty little bit of fluff. They intruded into my personal space, even grabbing my T-shirt front between thumb and forefinger, twisting it up to simulate nipples. I spoke to them openly and reasonably and tried to make conversation. Every time I took a calm step back, they immediately followed up. The two drunks really wanted me to take a swing at one of them, so that they could finish their liberty with a fag-bashing before returning to the ship.

Things were very tense. I turned my head to Abdul-Jabbar and quietly told him "Cour" (run). Abdul Jabbar couldn't speak English, but was well aware that something really heavy was taking place in that language. He vanished from just behind my elbow. I was relieved that he had bugged out. No use two of us getting thrashed. Being beaten up by multiple opponents was familiar to me, and I knew, while very unpleasant, the experience is survivable. I spent a few seconds getting myself used to the idea that I would be beat bloody, and resigned myself to that fact. My acceptance of the future brought an emotional liberation.

I knew from past experience that I would only get to throw a single punch before I was swarmed, and that I would only get that one punch if I swung first. The only satisfaction I would get from the evening would be landing that one solid blow - - - everything after would be only pain and blood.

The time had come when I had to do something other than just back up another step. The bleary, jeering eyes of my countrymen were only inches away from my own, and the liquor fumes of their breath choked me. Turning slightly right, I moved my right hand low and I closed my fist pulling it back.   But I bumped something with my elbow !   RATS, there, directly behind me, was Abdul Jabbar.   He hadn't run off, but had only moved out of my peripheral vision.  To his eternal credit, he stood by me in spite of the imminent threat of being beaten up by six foreigners. Two to six is HOPELESS odds in a street-fight. I hadn't accepted the idea that my young friend Abdul Jabbar would be injured, so my 'one good punch' plan was ruined.

I had a long-shot idea, and asked the most aggressive opponent, "What do you do on the Little Rock ?"    His piggy eyes regarded me suspiciously, confused by the change of subject, but admitted to me that he was Chief Bosun's Something-or-Other. "That sounds like an important position", I offered. Well, it was just as though I had flipped a switch inside his head. He stopped, puffed up slightly, and in a slurred voice began to expound to me JUST HOW important he was! Shortly he offered me a pull from his hip flask of liquor and slapped me on the back, allowing as how I didn't seem to be such a bad guy!! A few minutes later we parted regretfully, vowing eternal friendship, because they had to get back aboard by midnight.

So, against all odds, we did NOT get pounded into the pavement that night, and I learned an important lesson. Every aggressive asshole in the world is proud of something. If you can figure out what that something is, and express an interest in it, you cease to be a person who should be knocked down, and become someone to whom to brag. And once you make that crucial transition from "opponent" to "audience", belligerence just fades away. I have used this defensive technique twice since, and it has never yet failed me.

When my second Libyan transit visa was ready, I bid adieu to Abdul-Jabbar and his mother, thanking them for their kindness, and headed again southward towards Libya.

# MISSED CHANCES & MINOR MIRACLES IN LIBYA

At the border I filled out Libya's detailed currency declaration forms. Later the realization came that whenever a country demands currency declarations, it means that they have passed laws to legally cheat you by artificially inflating the value of their own currency. Crossing the border successfully after dark, I was given a free ride in a really packed dolmush (local share taxis, mostly Citroens) to the Libyan capital city of Tripoli, still several high-speed hours away. Also riding that dolmush was a nice young Tunisian guy who took me with him to the nasty tin shack lodging which he shared with five other Tunisian guest workers. They very kindly fed me and gave me the best bed in the crowded little dirt-floored slum. These guys all turned out to be Boy Scouts, so the Tunisian chapter of Baden Powell's international organization had welcomed me warmly into both Tunisia and Libya.

In the morning, as I prepared to push on eastward towards Egypt, my hosts took up a collection, and gave me five dinars, since they assumed I must be destitute. This was really a lot of money at the time, both to them and to me, and I tried and tried to refuse it, but finally accepted when they convinced me that to turn it away would be a big insult to them. The 5 dinars (about $20 USD) turned out to be more than I could spend in my four days in transit of Libya.

Tripoli itself was extremely boring. It was new and slick, and garish, and already crumbling around the edges. Most if not all of the shops were tackily beautified by too many strings of multicolored Christmas tree lights, imported from Europe. The whole place reeked of newly acquired oil-money vulgarity. I left Tripoli as quickly as I could.

Once out of the city, I soon learned that hitch-hiking in Libya is easier than anywhere else on this planet. There is really only one main road in Libya, of one lane in each direction, so all of the traffic in the country passes along it. I hitched easily across Libya from Tunisia into Egypt in four days, and never had to wait for a ride. As a matter of fact, after the first day, if I saw a truck coming towards me, I would hide from it, because I knew it would stop, and it was a slower ride than the next passenger car which would also stop and pick me up. I even had cars going the OTHER way stop and see if I had changed my mind and wanted to go back the way I had come. Everyone who picked me up compelled me to have a meal with them, so one day I had four lunches.

Libya's newfound wealth was everywhere apparent, and especially in the attitudes of some of the men who gave me lifts. They were very proud of their new automobiles, and usually also wanted me to admire their new fancy wristwatches. One guy riding in his friend's car when they picked me up proudly displayed the wallet photo of HIS car, just to demonstrate that he, too, was rich and important enough to own an auto. My first ride out of Tripoli was with a Libyan truck driver named Abduraman who spoke some English, having worked with American oil companies before they were thrown out of the country. It was a comfortable ride, proceeding all day long, at a slow but steady pace. I spent the time imagining that we were part of the supply system for the Afrika Korps back in 1941, bringing needed food from Tripoli to the Axis front lines. What a horrible, tenuous, long supply line it was!

## *Starlight Serenade*

When night descended we camped beside the road next to the truck, and cooked up a little communal dinner on my portable stove. After the food had been stowed, and Abduraman's prayers towards Mecca had been accomplished, he opened the truck window and turned on the radio softly to a whining middle-eastern music station. He then produced a double-barreled reeded flute, and sat outside on the ground, wrapping himself head to foot in a blanket. With a million stars gleaming overhead, he began to play, his own ethereal, floating, lonesome flute compositions accompanied by the equally strange Arabian music on the radio. It was a wonderful, other-worldly experience, the exotic music sounding somehow strangely familiar and comforting. The effect was somewhat spoiled later in the evening when Abduraman made a pass at me, but he seemed to take rejection well. So I missed out on a night of wild starlit passion among the romantic sand dunes. Late the next morning Abduraman dropped me by the road and turned off on a dirt side road to deliver his cargo. I hitched on eastward along the main highway.

## Short Circuit Miracle

That day I got a ride for 400 km in a Land rover with four passengers who proved to be policemen going to a conference. The highest-ranking official spoke good English, and they were all friendly to me, and easy to get along with. They stopped at a local police station and compelled the staff chef to fix us all a very nice lunch.

I had an experience during that ride, which still makes me smile when I think of it. The Land Rover in which we were traveling was brand-new, and still had the "new car" smell. Motoring down the highway, the engine would occasionally sputter and miss, and I noticed that the dashboard lights flickered in sympathy with the engine. There seemed to be some sort of an intermittent electrical short, and the problem became more frequent and more extreme as we progressed. Finally the engine cut out and died, started itself again for a few seconds, then again went dark and silent. The vehicle drifted to the shoulder of the road, a sandy plateau covered with small rocks.

Libyan Policemen

The four policemen got out and propped up the hood, peering inside with strangely incurious expressions on their faces. Then they all looked very expectantly at me, still standing at my place beside the rear door. Their faces eloquently said - "Well, Americans know everything there is to know about automobiles, so, what are you going to do about the problem?" Yowee, that was a stumper, for I have never been a motorhead. However, I do understand electrical systems in a general sort of way, and this was an electrical problem. But intermittent glitches are notoriously difficult or impossible to locate. So I walked forward towards the engine compartment, my brain furiously going through the cognitive process, all the while struggling to appear calm. "Well", I could hear myself thinking, "where should I start looking for an electrical problem which could be anywhere? I'll start at the battery." As I reached the front of the car, all the while observed closely by four pairs of eyes, I reached out and grasped the positive terminal of the battery. I was astonished to hear and feel a slight crackling pop!! Exactly there, just under my fingers, where the positive cable curved over the air cleaner bracket, the insulation had been worn away by the vibration of the engine!! I spent a moment hunting along the side of the road until I discovered a discarded plastic bag which I wound around the cable to re-insulate it from the metal bracket. The Rover started right up and ran perfectly for the remainder of the trip !!  Talk about luck !!

I didn't make any acknowledgment of success, not even a smile, but I could tell that the now-quiet Libyan police inspectors were impressed. They hadn't heard any of the discord going on inside my head. They had only seen the longhaired foreign freak walk confidently up to the engine compartment, place his hand immediately on the problem, and repair it promptly with a piece of roadside garbage. The policemen reached Benghazi, where I got down and rented one bed in a simple shoddy hotel room. Nothing much of interest in Benghazi, but I was quite a curiosity at the public baths that evening. The next morning I hiked out to the eastern edge of Benghazi town and again stuck out my thumb.

## "Remember the People of Palestine"

That day one of my four short rides was in an auto full of expatriate Palestinians. Two of them spoke French, and they were all very anti-American. Our interesting discussion centered around their question "Why does America Help the Jews". It didn't seem to be a rhetorical question, they appeared to be genuinely puzzled. Well, I had my own answer to that one, and explained it to them so it made sense.

For starters I told them that lots of the media in the United States is owned by Jews. Yep, they had heard that, and it made sense to them that this would help to lead public opinion. But they grew uneasy and resisted the course of my logic as I explained the more compelling reason. "If America didn't help the Jews," I said, "the Arabs would overrun them, don't you agree?" Yes, yes, they all agreed emphatically. "And, Israel has nuclear weapons ("le bombe atomique"), don't you agree?" No, they didn't agree at all with that, but after I pointed out that Israel had the scientists and the money and the technology and plenty of time to develop the Bomb, they finally grudgingly agreed that yes, probably there were nukes in Israel, but so what? "So, my friends, if America does not help Israel, and the Arabs overrun Israel, what happens when the first Iraqi tank clatters into Tel Aviv?"
Cairo > phhht!
Damascus > phhht!
Tripoli > phhht!
Baghdad > phhht!
Amman > phhht!

"To prevent this is the reason America supports Israel." There was a deep, contemplative silence in the car for many seconds. Finally one of the Palestinians said, softly, more to himself than to me, "Yes, that would be just like the Jews." As we parted company they exhorted me to "Remember the people of Palestine".

My fourth night in Libya I got down from an evening ride near a small village called Timimi, and walked towards the nearby Mediterranean. I figured a night sleeping on the sandy beach would be better than one on the hard ground. But in evening's half-light I had badly miscalculated the true distance to the sea. I marched for 30 minutes through muddy tidal-flats covered with salty bushes, before giving up. It was obvious that there would be no sandy beach, so I picked a local "high spot" which wasn't too soggy, and stretched out my plastic ground cover and sleeping bag. In the morning I had an unrewarding, half-hour-long slog back to the highway.

## Local Commander

One of my rides that day was in the vehicle of a uniformed high Libyan military officer who was traveling somewhere in the company of his brother. When they learned that I was American, the officer launched into a tirade against the American imperialists!! In the course of the next hour, I learned, among other things, that the Syrians had seven huge missiles which could hit Washington DC, that the United States government was offering a reward of 50 million dollars for Khadafi's death, and that the officer had just completed a series of maneuvers with his local militiamen which would enable them to throw the US Marine Corps back into the sea when they attempted the imminently-expected amphibious invasion. I tried and tried to talk to the guy, but he just was oblivious to any attempt at reason. I found that he had read most of the above horse-waste in a Lebanese magazine. I finally gave up trying to break through his impenetrable wall of bombastic dogma, deciding to simply hope our fearless leader wouldn't realize that I was a spy, sent to learn his top-secret counter-invasion plans. The historic fortress of Tobruk was only viewed from the high road as I motored past, not taking the turnoff to go and have a closer look.

# I almost Escape Libya

It proved difficult for me to spend any money in Libya. The one time I went into a store to buy a can-opener and some Chinese canned apples, the owner gave me everything I put on the counter for free, wouldn't accept payment. Men who gave me a ride assumed that I must be destitute, and often tried to give me money. Therefore including the 5 dinars forced on me by my Tunisian Boy Scout friends, I had more money going out of Libya than coming in, which caused problems at the outgoing border crossing. Not being an experienced overlander at the time, having only been on the road for a few months, I showed the extra money and my currency declaration form to the Libyan border official. - - - Mistake. - - - He believed my story of where it had come from, but said "This is very irregular! You must go down the hall and speak with Mr. Raisa !" So I went back down the hall, straight back out the Libyan door, walked 500 yards back into Libya, 100 yards out into the night-time desert, and went to sleep behind a bush for eight hours, until I was sure that the shifts had changed at the border post.

# LAND OF THE PHARAOHS

In the early morning I went through customs hiding the extra money, and all went well. I was in Egypt ! The Egyptian border guards compelled a dolmush driver to take me the short distance down over the face of the famous Sollum escarpment, with many switch-backs, to the tatty seaside village of the same name. It was there in Sollum that I first encountered one of the strange differences between the culture of the western world, and that of Egypt.

Unsophisticated Egyptians have no social taboo against staring! Many times, in Egypt I found that to stop walking, or try to just sit on a wall for a moment caused the quick formation of a dense crowd of young Egyptian men standing in a tight semicircle around me, the nearest about three feet away, all staring at me intently, generally without speaking. Occasionally, if one of my new admirers was bold and knew a few of words of English, he would tell me all three of them. As I debarked in Sollum this behavior manifested with a vengeance. There were about 120 young Egyptian men standing around in the morning, obviously with nothing to do, and they immediately crowded around me, as the most interesting thing they had seen in a LONG time. I talked to them in simple English, and found that we could not communicate. I talked to them in simpler Arabic, and found that they did not parse my sounds as a language they should understand. I resolved at that moment to learn lots more Arabic, and began collecting words and phrases in my journal, practicing at every opportunity.

## Frisbee as a Second Language

Well, since language wasn't working to communicate, I knew another way, and pulled out my Frisbee. Frisbee as a second language was an immediate success. I gestured that I was going to throw it several times, and thought the crowd understood, but when I did fly it towards the nearby onlookers, they dove out of its path in terror!! Obviously this was the very first frisbee any of them had ever seen. I followed the toy and picked it up, and did the trick of flying it up at a 45 degree angle, hard and fast out over the beach sand, then catching it when it stalled and descended rapidly back towards me. This caused a huge stir, and lots of comment. Pretty soon I had one of the braver Egyptian lads learning to hold and throw the toy, and after that everyone wanted to try it out. I sat on the sea-wall laughing as the big scrum of young men stampeded back and forth along the beach. Occasionally my frisbee would wobble up out of the center of the mass, to be snatched out of the air by many hands, all of which would tussle for it enthusiastically, to be the one lucky enough to launch it on its next wobbly flight. I know it sounds like a wild exaggeration, but I swear on my mother's eyes that there were over 100 guys playing with my frisbee simultaneously. People were getting trampled in the mess.

I pulled my little viewfinder camera out of its heavy leather belt pouch to try to record the scene. This was even more interesting than the frisbee, and the crowd immediately surged around me again, each young man determined to be in the center of the photo. I marched out onto the beach and my crowd backed up ahead of me. When I got them far enough out, I tried everything I could think of to get them to understand that I wanted them to stay there so I could get a photo of the whole crowd together, but every time I took a step back, 120 people took one step towards me. I finally gave up and snapped a photo of a tiny segment of the mass of Egyptian manhood. To my amazement, when the dolmush was ready to leave, my frisbee magically appeared from the crowd and was given back to me. I had already given it up for "adopted".

I rode the dolmush to the dirty little seaside town of Mersa Matrouh, where there was a comfortable youth hostel, settling down there for three nights to rest up and do laundry, etc. The weather was a little bit too chilly for swimming, but I sat in the wan sunshine a lot, and wrote letters. Most of the guests in the dormitory beds were Egyptians, some of whom spoke English, so I worked hard on my Arabic.

## Memories of 1956

Arriving in Egypt, I was a bit apprehensive that the people would react badly to Americans, since the US supported Egypt's enemy, Israel. I was pleased to find that at the time, America was VERY popular with the average Egyptian. Whenever Egyptians heard my nationality, they broke into broad smiles, welcomed me enthusiastically to their country, and told me that they really loved America and her people. After some confusion, I discovered the non-intuitive reason. The average Egyptian's psyche harked back to the Suez incident of 1956 when Britain, France, and Israel colluded in a short, violent military campaign which snatched the Suez canal from Egypt with very flimsy moral justification. America's diplomatic intervention on Egypt's behalf had compelled the aggressive forces to return the canal to Egypt, and that incident was still strong and current in the minds of the Egyptians, in spite of everything which had taken place in the interim.

The third morning following, I was hitching just to the east of Mersa Matrouh when the first dolmush stopped for me. It was a Citroen station-wagon type, and was already packed with about nine people and all their luggage. I smiled and waved him on, saying in Arabic "free ride". But that's what the dolmush driver intended, and he shoe-horned me somehow into the luggage area in back, doubled over, with a small piece of side-window to peer through, agreeing to take me all the way to Alexandria for free! We drove steadily for a couple of hours, and then slowed down. I couldn't believe my eyes !! Lined up along both sides of the road were dozens of German, Italian, British and American derelict tanks, armored cars, and artillery pieces!! I have always been fascinated by military history, and especially by armored fighting vehicles, so I hollered to the driver that I had changed my mind and was stopping here. The cabbie graciously pulled over to disentangle me from the luggage and drop me off. I wandered among the rusty armor starry-eyed!

A sign informed me that I was at El Alamein, site of the turning-point battle in the struggle for North Africa in the Second World War. The Egyptian army had dragged lots of 35-year-derelict vehicles out of the farther reaches of the desert and lined them up on both sides of the road. A small three-room military museum squatted at the far end of the display. I talked with the young Egyptian lieutenant in charge of the six-man museum staff, who fortunately spoke excellent English. He informed me that the railhead of El Alamein was still some distance away, and that there was nothing "here" except the museum. I was the only museum visitor that day.

I spent a very pleasant late morning and early afternoon climbing all over and through the historic vehicles, inspecting the obvious battle damage. They hadn't been cleaned up at all, just dragged in and left there, and so were full of windblown sand, with bits of shattered periscope glass, weathered paper, and rotted rubber in the bottoms of the fighting compartments. It was like being transported by time machine back 35 years, because the dry climate had preserved the vehicles themselves very well. Some of them were mislabeled, but I decided not to try to convince the museum staff to correct their little identifying plaques. I took a dozen snapshots of the rusting relics.

El Alamein

# The Perils of the Western Desert

My friend the lieutenant invited me to have lunch with his garrison. It was a good opportunity for him to gain status with them by showing off his English, and translating whatever I said. They were amazed to hear that I had slept out in the open desert.

"How did you do this, Mr. Chick ?"

So I opened my backpack, and on the museum floor laid out my plastic ground-sheet, and sleeping bag, and explained how I put my boots next to my head, with my little flashlight in the top of my boots. The soldiers all muttered and shook their heads in disbelief. I asked my host what they were saying.

"Mr. Chick, we cannot believe that you sleep this way with no protection in such a dangerous place." When I told them that there was nothing to be afraid of out in the desert, they dissented strongly. I demanded to know what I should fear.

"Tigers !" was the heartfelt reply.

That was my first encounter with an interesting cultural glitch which I later confirmed. In America we think of the Arabs as people who are at home in the desert. Nothing could be farther from the truth. Perhaps 99.9% of the local populations are "village Arabs" who are scared SPITLESS of the desert. It is only a very few true Bedouin who feel at home in those open spaces. I'm sure Arab mothers all over the middle east use the mythical desert tigers as a tool to terrify their little ones, and as a result, the whole culture believes implicitly that the clean open desert is a very perilous place. I told this story to my Israeli friends in 1999, and they all agreed, "YEAH, there are tigers out there in the desert, those Egyptians were right!", which makes me think that Israeli mothers use the same fables.

## Ancient Alexandria

Hitch hiking to Alexandria along the south shore of the Mediterranean was easy. I located the well-concealed youth hostel in the late evening. Alexandria, formerly the center of civilization throughout the Mediterranean world, had always attracted me. I went searching for any remaining traces of the ancient Pharos lighthouse, one of the seven wonders of the ancient world, and the Library of Alexandria, the storehouse of all ancient recorded knowledge. Medieval Pashas had constructed a fortification named Quait Bey on the outer edge of Alexandria harbor where the Pharos lighthouse had stood until it was toppled by a massive earthquake in the dark ages. Stones from the Pharos were believed to have been re-used in building the fortification, but I was disappointed that effectively nothing remained of the lighthouse itself. (Recent underwater surveys of the sea and harbor floor in the area have identified large stones and statues which must have been pieces of the lighthouse. That work is ongoing.) I visited Quait Bey which then housed the interesting Egyptian Naval museum. It may be the only naval museum on earth displaying a number of 4000-year-old models of equally ancient ship designs. The famous Library of Alexandria, which tragically burned in Roman times, similarly left no remaining trace in the modern city.

## Politics, Religion, and Sex

Everywhere I went in Alex I attracted crowds of staring young male Egyptian followers. I couldn't stop for a moment to admire the view because of the mass of people who would immediately congregate. After most of a day of this it began to be annoying. Many of these young guys spoke some English, and wanted to try it out. Quite a few times a day I was invited to discuss the same three fascinating subjects, Middle Eastern politics, comparative religion, and sex. Especially sex.

The Egyptians had heard that western women were much easier to get to know than Egyptian women, and they wanted to hear ALL about that. Several times that day young Egyptian men proudly displayed photos of their western girlfriends. The first one showed a pudgy blonde gal with her arm around the proud photo-owner. But there was something a little strange about the picture, the whole side of it away from the Egyptian guy was snipped off. Well, I didn't think much of it until hours later when I was shown a similarly trimmed picture of an Egyptian beau beside a dark-haired German lass. Then I realized the scam. These had been photos of western couples who had agreed to be photographed with the local boys, who had subsequently cut the European boyfriends out of the picture. This trick almost made it appear that the lady in question had been the photo-trimmer's girlfriend. I wonder if the rather obvious subterfuge fooled even any of the immediate friends of those pseudo-lotharios.

Another cross-cultural feature which caught my attention were the pairs of Egyptian men walking around the city hand in hand. At first it was disorienting to see two mature, uniformed, battle-scarred Egyptian sergeants walking down the esplanade, holding hands, looking dreamily into one another's eyes, obviously deeply in love. After getting used to the idea, however, I found it rather sincere and charming. I realized that it was my western culture which was messed up about guys holding hands with one another, and that the Egyptians had it right. (Returning to Egypt many years later in 1997, western-cultural mores had apparently won out, and I saw no pairs of men holding hands in public.)

# A vagabond's guide to Cairo

The Egyptian railways are cheap and efficient, so I rode as a paying passenger through the fertile Nile delta southward to Cairo. The Victorian-appearing railway station welcomed me, and soon the public buses took me across the city to the neighborhood of the big, impersonal, dusty Beet Shebab, where I took a dormitory bed. Cairo's ramshackle, fume-belching buses were a curious mode of transport. There were 10 piaster, 2 piaster, and 1 piaster buses all following the same routes. At the time, a piaster was worth less than two US cents. The less expensive buses were obviously subsidized by the government. The two and one-piaster buses were universally JAMMED with humanity, at all times of the day. The windows of these buses had no glass in them, and young men would sit with legs hanging out of every window. To board the bus was a claustrophobic experience requiring substantial bodily strength and determination, with people jammed against you on every side. The fee collectors spent their days physically forcing themselves down the center aisle and demanding piasters from the passengers. It was common for a rider hanging out of a window to jump off when a fee was demanded, and run alongside for a block, then jumping back up to the window-sill perch when the fee collector had passed on down the bus. I kept my valuables well secured and concealed in my neck pouch, because there was no other way one could protect them from pickpockets in such a chaotic situation.

## Disciples

Cairo was crowded, bustling, and very dirty. Strolling around the city, I met a group of nice young Coptic Christian men, one of whom spoke workable English. We walked around together most of the afternoon, and I heard all about the discrimination by the Muslim majority against the Copts. Additional subjects were again, Middle Eastern Politics, Comparative Religion, and Sexual Opportunity. My curious new friends asked me at one point.

"But now you will please tell us, Mister Chick, how many times YOU ficki-fick ?!?"

I was taken aback, but it seemed to be a serious question, so instead of trying to explain that in my culture one just doesn't ask such questions, and that a gentleman would decline to answer, I did a quick calculation in my head and gave them a conservative number which would not have even raised eyebrows in California. I was truly taken aback when my honest answer was greeted with universal derision and disbelief! None of those frustrated, virginal, hormone-packed guys would credit the truth, and all took me for a transparent liar.

My Coptic Disciples

I never made that mistake again. In future when I was asked for details about my own familiarity with females, I politely declined to answer. I am certain that my reticence was interpreted as an attempt to artificially inflate my macho status through an aura of mystery. Whenever that question arose, it was impossible to win. I had to choose between being thought either a liar or a poseur.

## *Pyramids of Giza*

As with most tourists, I quickly found my way across the Nile to visit the pyramids. I fully expected the great pyramid to be impressive, but in spite of this, it took my breath away the first time I saw it close-up. The legions of persistent touts and trinket sellers were an annoyance, but the ancient monument, the ONLY one of the seven wonders of the ancient world still standing, is a true soul-opener. I walked all around Cheops' great pyramid, and paid an extra admission fee to climb inside along with all of the bus tourists. It was a great experience, and I am awfully glad that I didn't miss it. The king's chamber in the heart of Cheops pyramid is one of the most mysterious and interesting places on earth, and to have come to within a few hundred feet of it and not entered would have been unthinkable. I visited the Sphinx which is very close-by, and decided to come back another day to see the "sound and light" show after dark. The vagabond-telegraph knew that the "son et Lumiere" show could be enjoyed for free by anyone willing to sit on the ground outside the "official" area of chairs prepared for the paying package tourists.

Chick & Cheops

When I did return to the pyramids, I discovered something else about them. It is impossible to carry away in one's mind the impression of how HUGE they really are. Having visited only a few days previously, I still was stunned anew by their mass and unbelievable antiquity !! It was as though I were again experiencing them for the first time. On my third visit several days later, I was for the third time boggled by the scale those ancient monuments.

The morning after my first visit to the pyramids I visited the Egyptian Archaeological Museum. It is completely amazing, with so many exhibits, and such an abundance of archaeological treasure that I couldn't take it all in on the initial visit. King Tut's golden mask and sarcophagus were touring the world at the time, so I didn't get to see those relics, but I was captivated by Tut's throne, with the delicate inlaid pictures of Tut and his sister/wife gently touching one another. In my opinion it is the greatest artistic treasure on earth. While wandering in the museum I met Antonio, who I hadn't seen since the Tunisian border. It was good to talk with him. I repaid him one Tunisian dinar's worth of Egyptian pounds for the loan he supplied when I found myself with no Tunisian money at the frontier, compelled to reverse course for a new Libyan visa.

## Cairo's Citadel

Above Cairo sits the old citadel, a medieval fortress which has been rebuilt and reworked many times over the centuries. Major Citadel attractions are two beautiful old mosques, the Muhammad Ali and the An Nasr, as well as the Egyptian War museum. Riding the two piaster bus to near the citadel, I arrived in an area of many huge old mosques at the base of the hill. Nearly every ruler of Cairo throughout the Muslim centuries had built a mosque for his own funerary monument, and in this area they were very thick. I climbed the historic entry ramp to the fortification.

The Mohammed Ali mosque at the summit of Cairo's citadel is the largest and most breath-taking, with an immense interior space and four slender minarets at the corners. I took off my shoes (and tipped the attendants to mind them) in order to enter. Both mosques are beautiful inside and out. The glorious architecture is somewhat spoiled by the mosque authorities, who clutter up the huge interior volumes of both structures with innumerable chains and cables and hanging lamps. Mosques were an excellent sanctuary from the gangs of talkative young Egyptians. When sitting on a mosque floor in quiet contemplation, no one would accost me.

The War Museum on the Citadel grounds was fascinating. Visiting in 1975, shortly after the 1973 war, the whole first floor of the museum was devoted to the recent heroism of the Egyptian soldiers while fighting the Israelis. The display had a slap-dash hurriedly thrown together feeling to it, very jingoistic and self-congratulatory. Outside in the courtyard of the museum were displayed a half-dozen destroyed Israeli vehicles, and a couple of shot-down Israeli jets. Inside I examined captured Israeli equipment, including such trophies as a civilian Zenith television set, Israeli military issue sun- block creme, and a genuine Israeli telephone pole.

Egyptian authorities took a clever position at the end of the 1973 war. The Egyptian public at large was never told that, militarily, they lost that war. Nobody in Egypt had heard, or would believe, that the Israelis came back across the canal, encircled Suez city on the Egyptian side, and cut off huge numbers of out-of-supply Egyptian units before Kissinger's diplomacy stopped the fighting. This was smart because it later allowed the Egyptians to make peace at Camp David without losing face at home. The Egyptian man-in-the-street believed that they had whipped the Israelis in '73, and therefore could negotiate from a morally superior position. In essence, the false victory facade allowed Egypt make peace before actually winning a war. Once I realized the implications, I also supported that fiction, keeping my mouth shut about the true situation at the end of the '73 conflict.

After a night in the soul-less youth hostel in Cairo, much better lodging, only slightly more expensive than the Beet Shebab, presented itself. I moved into the nice run-down, centrally-located Pensione Roma where I had my own room stuffed with heavy antique furniture, my own sink, and a bathroom down the hall with unlimited hot water for only $2 per night!! It was luxury, and I really enjoyed my stay there. Bath water was heated on demand, not stored. When the hot water tap was turned, a pilot light ignited a big group of gas burners, and these directly heated a series of exposed serpentine copper pipes through which the water flowed immediately before it issued from the tap. It seemed like a good (if not energy efficient ?) system, and certainly worked very well.

Eating in Egypt was easy and inexpensive for a vagabond. I became enamored with Egyptian "street vendor" foods, especially a starchy concoction called Kusheri. For only five cents the pushcart vendor would shovel lots of little pieces of warm pasta, some cooked lentils, sometimes rice, and sometimes even fried onions into a bowl and dribble a thin, tasty red sauce over the mixture. It was good, and filling, and great value. I ate Kusheri almost every day, often more than once.

My Coptic disciples had made me aware of the suppressed Christian community in Egypt. I went to visit some wonderful, remarkably-old Coptic churches in the shabbier quarters of Cairo. They were low and thick-walled, not at all like the amazing elegant tall mosques of the city. Seemed almost as though they had been built with an eye to defense. While being given a tour of one ancient church I learned that the Copts claim to have invented movable paintings. Up to the early Muslim era in Egypt paintings had always been done directly on walls, as murals. The Egyptian Christians, finding that their churches were burned in pogroms every couple of generations, decided to create their sacred paintings on gessoed boards which could be removed and hidden during troubled times, and re-hung on the church walls after the buildings had been repaired and re-painted. I was shown one of the oldest movable paintings in the world, a dark-ages image on cedar wood of Christ.

# *Khamsin*

While in Cairo I was treated to a Khamsin, the occasional hot, dry desert winds from the west. That Khamsin took the form of a powerful dust storm, and turned the entire sky, horizon to horizon, a strange pale orange color from the quantities of desert dust in the air. People went about the streets of Cairo with handkerchiefs over their mouths and noses, and kept their windows closed to try to keep out the dust. That dust went everywhere and was abrasive and gritty between my neck and my collar. Fortunately the Khamsin lasted less than two days, and the skies cleared again.

At the height of the Khamsin I met a Canadian vagabond named Bill on the street. We peered at each other through dusty eye-slits, conversed, and became friends. Bill was unenthused with the Beet Shebab, so with the permission of the staff, I moved him in onto the floor of my comfortable pensione room. Soon poor Bill became quite ill with gut-gripes, so he inherited the bed, and I sat with him and ran errands for him until he recovered. We met again later in Aswan, and much later in Nairobi.

Bill had already scouted Cairo's American University, and took me to visit the inexpensive cafeteria, as well as to meet some English-speaking Muslim women. We chatted up three lovely young ladies at the adjacent table, and had a nice conversation. They were all from Saudi Arabia, and in order to allow them to attend the American university without compromising their reputations, all three of their entire families, parents, brothers, and sisters, had also moved to Cairo to chaperone them!! Yowee. It must be nice to be born rich. The American university was the only place in all of the Middle East where I managed to speak openly with young Muslim women, who traditionally are jealously guarded and kept separate from males, and from other polluting influences.

Riding local buses I took a day trip south some distance to Sakkara, to see the ancient monuments there. Pharaoh Djoser's step pyramid is the world's first monumental stone building, and very impressive, though not very beautiful. In some nearby derelict tombs, a guard encouraged me to take a piece of 5000 year old wrapping linen from a partial mummy which was resting in a corner. That seemed too disrespectful an act to me, so I declined. This experience brought into sharp focus another of my mistaken assumptions. I had always believed that in ancient Egypt the wealthy and important people were mummified and placed in tombs on the West side of the Nile. Actually, for several thousand years, EVERYBODY was mummified and placed in tombs in that area !! The whole place is just honeycombed with tombs, and bones and bits of mummies are very common only a few yards away from the maintained tourist paths. At Sakkara I had a piece of luck. Returning past Djoser's step pyramid I encountered a group of French-speaking bus tourists. Since the local buses were uncomfortable, and a substantial hassle to ride, I accosted the cute young French tour leader, and asked her if I could ride with them back to Central Cairo. My stumbling, ungrammatical French was apparently sufficient, because she agreed, but first specified that I would accompany them while they visited the Pyramids of Giza, and then the papyrus institute. Sounded fine to me, and things worked out very well. There were plenty of French folk who weren't curious about the inner passages of Kephren's pyramid, the second-largest, so I went inside with the tour party for free. The French group tourists were quite interested in me, and asked lots of questions about solo vagabonding in North Africa. I parted from them that evening at the Nile Hilton and walked back to Pensione Roma.

When sated with the sights and attractions of Cairo, the railway carried me south up the Nile to Luxor, where a cheap dormitory in a back-street vagabond hotel welcomed me. In and near Luxor are two massive reconstructed pharaonic temples, while on the west side of the Nile is the Valley of the Tombs of the Kings. The huge, confusing complex of the temple of Karnak, nicely rebuilt, showed areas of the original color still adhering to the decorated undersides of a few of the massive lintels! I wonder just how long ago that paint was applied. Every surface exposed to the direct sun had long ago been bleached of all color.

Crossing the Nile on the cheap ferry (there is a bridge today) the hordes of dragomen, touts and donkey-drovers were eluded with some difficulty. I took an all-day self-guided walking tour of the Valley of the Kings, Queen Hapshetsut's temple, and the Colossi of Memnon.

## Fury trumps Judgment

As I was coming out of my Luxor freak lodging in the early morning, I encountered a young Canadian couple in the cramped reception area, just hanging out. When I approached they asked where I was going, My target was Edfu temple, south on the railway, and across the Nile, and they asked if they could come along. I was used to this behavior in pairs or triples of unescorted women in Egypt. Egyptian men could be a real hassle to western ladies walking around by themselves. I was powerful and fit and reasonably sane at the time, and I realized that they just wanted some THING to keep the unsophisticated Egyptian guys a little farther away. It had nothing to do with me as a person, I was being recruited as an escort-object only.

Now John, the Canadian husband, was a tall, strong guy, and I figured he could probably do just fine at escort by himself, but along I went. I was wrong. His wife, Kay, was little, and plump-pear-shaped, with a broad, soft bottom, and had long wavy FLAME RED Scottish hair. Even though she had it tied back, it was a PROBLEM. At the time the Egyptians made their women put that stiff henna crap in their hair to make it sort of muddy brown/red. Kay was perfect in every male eye!! The unsophisticated guys would get that "radar lock" stare, and approach directly with the full intent of touching and grabbing her. It happened once every few minutes!! Yowee!! With me walking on one side, and John on the other, keeping our bodies between Kay and the would-be assailants, threatening bodily harm, we were just barely keeping her un-grabbed. Tense, it was, and not a very fun situation. I finally convinced Kay to stick her hair down her blouse and put a scarf over her head, which helped some but didn't stop the strange behavior. I asked John "What could those guys possibly be thinking ?!?!" He said he had been pondering that question for a week, and had finally figured it out.

According to John, when an Egyptian male sees Kay, inside his head he says "- - - - WOW !!! - - - - I can have sex with her!!!!!!! - - - - - - - - - and I'm going to try RIGHT NOW !"

In my heart, I knew he must be correct. No other theory fits the data. But this generates the next question: WHY do these men imagine that western women will immediately go knees-up when unescorted? Polling many people, I have culled two possible explanations. I spent one evening at the apartment of an American-educated Egyptian whom I met in Cairo, mostly discussing Middle East politics. He attributed the obnoxious behavior to the many American movies which play in Egypt. In any given American movie there is a good chance that at some point in the story the female lead will go to bed with somebody to whom she is not married. This is particularly true of the movies which are selected to be dubbed into Arabic and released in Egypt. And this is never the case in movies produced in Arab countries. According to my informant, the unsophisticated Egyptian males GET the fact of the bed games out of wedlock, but MISS the fact that it is necessary to the plot. Therefore they convince themselves that all western women walk around continually ready to hop into bed with the first guy who feels them up.

My friend Gene, who lived for years in Egypt and went to school there has another interesting take on the question. He found that on the rare occasions that the stifling chaperoning system broke down, the Egyptian young ladies were quite willing to "fool around", to a limited extent, with available young men. They didn't seem to be too worried about maintaining their own virtue, believing that to be the responsibility of the chaperones. If this is generally true, then Egyptian men, seeing a western woman un-chaperoned, would conclude that she would behave similarly. In spite of my respect for Gene's opinion, I have a suspicion that his experience was strongly slanted by the circumstance of his own good looks and undeniable personal charm. Neither of these explanations satisfies me, and neither explains the behavior towards the HEAVILY escorted Canadian cutie of our story. So, ultimately, I still don't understand the Egyptian grope artists, and am still seeking additional data.

The Canadians and I rode to Edfu and deposited my backpack at the railway office. We walked over the new (at the time) Nile bridge, enjoyed the wonderfully-preserved ancient temple, and were returning to the Eastern side. The tall, modern bridge was very crowded, with autos, bikes, ox-carts, trucks, and plenty of pedestrians going both ways. My defensive position was on the inside, next to the wheeled traffic, and I was edgy, my supply of emotional harmony worn very thin. I saw an old bicycle coming the other way, and the teenage pilot went "Radar Lock Joy Face" when he saw Kay, veering through oncoming traffic towards her. I had Achmed covered, never taking my eyes off of him, and keeping a solid defensive screen. Problem was that behind me Kay and John had stopped without my knowing it, and I had continued to move forward OUT OF POSITION ! The weenie pedaled past and grabbed Kay hard by the breast on the way ! I was simply CRUSHED, as I had failed in my protective role.

Then he leered back over his shoulder with a smug expression. That did it. My emotions went from as low as I have ever felt to more angry than I have ever been, all in a heartbeat. WAAAARGH!! I went completely ballistic, berserk with fury, sprinting after him, blind with a purple rage behind my eyes. I'm not fast, and he should have escaped, but he was going against traffic until he could get to the other side of the road, and that slowed him substantially. After a short chase through the crowd, I locked a right hand grip of iron through the funny book-clamp-thing on the bike's rear fender. It hurt my fingers severely, but I would have lost fingers before I let go. Dragged him to a halt!!!

Now this felaheen knew from the look in my eyes that death was extremely near. He started to wail, and tried to jump off the bike, but made a bad mistake by choosing the right side away from me, which he had not practiced. Achmed got tangled up in the bike, and fell down on his back, partly under it, with me crawling up to kneel on top of his legs and seize him by his lapels! He was continuously screaming full volume now, begging Allah to save him, and his eyes were stark with genuine terror. One of those instant twenty-faces-deep-all-around Egyptian crowds materialized, each of the hundreds of watchers fascinated by the exciting drama being played out in front of them!! Well, now that I had him, WHAT was I going to do with him???? I was beginning to calm down now, and was no longer 100%-out-of-control-homicidal. I actually had a decision point, for the first time in many seconds.

My immediate impulse, triggered by my extra 'Y' chromosome, was to loosen Achmed's greasy brown teeth with my Yankee fist-of-retribution. I broke his grip on my right wrist, and pulled the fist back ready to smash his screaming face in, but somehow, I just couldn't do it. I considered tossing him over the bridge rail into the Nile, but the chances were excellent that he could not swim, and would drown. What was I gonna do, there at center stage? ? ?

Then came one of those rare, perfect Epiphanies which are given to mortal men only once or twice in a lifetime. I knew what to do. My left hand gripped his throat as I scooted partly off of him, rammed my claw-like fingers up between his thighs, and powerfully groped and molested and pinched and twisted his private parts!!! His eyes got huge, and he and the horrified crowd went COMPLETELY SILENT! I released him, tried to straighten up, but remained squatting off-balance, and held up my thumb and forefinger vertically about 1" apart. The crowd GOT IT, and laughed uproariously, with amusement mixed with relief!!! The glaringly red-faced dweeb went slithering away, dragging his pox-ridden bicycle with him. So on that day I was permitted to deliver JUSTICE, which is a very rare commodity. I'm sure there were folks in the crowd that knew the guy, and they certainly still tell the tale of Achmed being molested and humiliated by the Farangi. And I'll bet he never again groped a tourist gal.

That night I reached the lovely Nile-side town of Aswan, soon purchasing a ticket on the bi-weekly steamer south on Lake Nasser, heading deep into Darkest Africa.

# Sailing Lake Nasser

The ferry consisted of three barges strapped side by side, the center one having the engine and steering equipment, with a huge rough-plank-built paddle wheel at the stern.. Each of the outside barges held one well-used auto. There was a nice permanent awning over the heavy steel deck plates of the center barge where I spent most of my time, sitting and sleeping on the deck. There were not too many folks on the ferry, about 30, almost all of them Sudanese camel breeders who had taken their herds of camels north across the Nubian Desert and sold them for meat in Egypt. These guys were returning to the Sudan, carrying their camel saddles, and lots of "stuff" they had bought in Egypt and were taking home. Pretty hard lot, they were. Very black, wearing loose fitting cotton robes and head-cloths, each one with a wicked double-edged knife up his loose sleeve on a thong around his left biceps. It was a bit unnerving to have them do a quick chop with an empty left hand and have it suddenly filled with a weapon ready to be drawn. I found them quite friendly, and used my 20 words of Arabic on them, and we got along famously, sharing food, etc.

Shrine across the Nile

The ferry trip took two days and two nights, traveling through a really strange moonscape. There was almost no vegetation along the banks of Lake Nasser, the water coming right up to orange/yellow rocks and sand on both sides. Never got out of sight of at least one shore. Unfortunately we passed the amazing monuments at Abu Simbel on a moonless night, so I didn't get to see them. (Finally got to see Abu Simbel 22 years later when I took my parents to Egypt as a retirement present.)

# REMOTE SUDAN

Early morning of the third day we arrived at Wadi Halfa, in the Sudan. What a hole. A few nasty crumbling buildings and a run down railway terminus. Very hot and humid, of course, so close to the lake. And infested with flies, flies, and more flies! History buffs may recall that the Mahdi's head is supposed to be buried secretly somewhere at Wadi Halfa, but the original site of the town is now submerged under Lake Nasser. I cleared perfunctory customs, got my passport stamped, and bought a fourth class ticket on the train across the Nubian desert to Khartoum. Train (and ferry, for that matter) only ran twice a week. Yes, they DID have first, second, third, and fourth class carriages. The fourth class one had wooden slat benches and no transparent windows, only heavy wooden shutters, always left open. Now, it was hot and close and smelly in the carriages, and those Sudanese in the "know" climbed up on top of the carriages and sat on the roof. I followed.

After a few times it was easier to scramble up there from between the carriages, hanging grimly on to random pipes and fittings for support. No ladder or side-rails or any safety features on the roof, of course. It was much nicer up there as long as I kept my head covered from the punishing sun. Breezier and a much better view, and only occasionally did the coal-burning loco drop ashes on us.

## Nubian Desert

Everyone on top sat on the ridge-line facing right or left, with feet slightly lower on the curving carriage roof. The train stopped several times per day, but only for the five daily Muslim prayer times or to take on boiler water at one of the God-forsaken watering depots. There was no other reason to stop, as the Nubian desert is THE most desolate that I have ever witnessed, and I have seen quite a few deserts. Not a tree, not a bush, not a blade of grass. It was so dry and desolate that there were not even any bugs or flies once away from Wadi Halfa!! Quite amazing.

The railway line itself was well enough maintained. One strange feature did catch my attention. For hundreds of miles we passed regular holes dug into the desert along the railway line, each one about 12 feet long, eight feet wide, and two feet deep, with vertical walls and square top edges, and a 20 foot gap to the next one. I spent quite a while trying to figure out who had been doing so much digging recently. It was a shock when I finally realized that those holes had been dug by British Army Engineers in 1898 when they originally built the railway !! They were dug to procure the ballast on which the rails were laid, slightly higher than the surrounding desert. There is so little rain (less than 1 cm per year) out there that the holes hadn't "weathered" at all in the preceding 77 years, and actually looked like they had been dug the previous week!    (History buffs will remember that this is the railway Kitchener built to keep his forces supplied on the expedition to punish the Mahdist Sudanese for killing Chinese Gordon.)

It was two days and one night to Khartoum. I slept on the roof with everyone else. It was a little unnerving, because I figured I might roll off, down the sloping roof, but we all just lay crossways, legs on one side of the peak and head on the other, and things were fine. It got pretty darn cold at night, out there in the desert, in spite of the very high daytime temperatures. I put on my flannel shirt and jacket. When I awoke freezing in the early hours, I found out that all of my Sudanese camel-herder "buddies" had quietly moved behind me on the roof, and that I was at that moment the official cold-wind-break for the whole sleeping lot of them. Clever buggers. I quietly stepped over each of them in turn to the rear end of the carriage roof, spending the rest of the night with them breaking the frigid wind for me. The stars were just extraordinary, way out there away from any ambient earth-light. Just before dawn as I looked north, I watched the pole star slip below the horizon.

## Khartoum

Waking cold and stiff on top of the rumbling southbound train I found that we were once again in semi-fertile land along the Nile river. Later that day the train from Wadi Halfa arrived in Khartoum, and I went walking to try to find affordable lodging. But first, of course, I had to see the confluence of the Blue and White Niles, the "raison d'être" for Khartoum. I marched there, carrying my backpack. The White Nile, flowing out of Darkest Africa, was definitely pale chocolate brown, and the Blue, flowing down from the Ethiopian highlands, was a different color, less brown, but certainly a long stretch to call it blue. Across the river, on the Omdurman side, I could see the white dome of the Mahdi's tomb. Although it is empty, (the Mahdi's bones having been thrown into the river and the skull sent up the Nile as a macabre present for Victoria by Kitchener) it still attracted some Sudanese pilgrims and a few tourists like me. Big parts of Khartoum, at the time, were not too filthy, but in May, in the afternoon, the place gets REALLY hot. You can see heat shimmer on every street.

I finally found the youth hostel in Khartoum. It was two low dormitory buildings, without screens, and a dusty packed-earth courtyard with a high wall encircling it. Unfortunately, I found that Egyptian students, exiled to Khartoum because they couldn't get into a better school, lived in the youth hostel year-around. They had permanently booked every bed, ignoring the "rules" of the international youth hostel association. So I checked in anyway, my bed being a dusty piece of the hard-as-iron courtyard. After dusk the mosquitoes were quite a problem, as, in the open courtyard, my burning mosquito coils were not too effective. There were a few other young overland vagabonds sleeping on the ground in the courtyard, a Canadian couple, and an Irish lawyer. I stayed in Khartoum for about a week.

Khartoum doesn't have too many sites of historical interest. The confluence, the Mahdi's tomb, and the palace stairs where Gordon Pasha is claimed to have been killed (they are actually much too new) complete the list. Having seen them, I needed to decide which way to head. I knew that I eventually wanted to see the East African game parks, and the coast, and the amazing historical sites in Ethiopia, and I wanted to ride the Nile steamer. Since the steamer between Khartoum and Juba, in deep southern Sudan, was said to take up to 7 days with the current, and up to 11 days against the current, I decided to ride it north, "with" the current. To accomplish this I needed to go overland to Juba, near the Ugandan border, and then ride the steamer through the world's largest swamp, the Sudd, and then back to Khartoum.

Khartoum was, however, an interesting town for people watching. It is just about exactly the crossover point between the northern Semitic Arabic-speaking Muslims and the southern Black African Animists/Christians. The Sudanese black Muslims in that region are, as a class, the BIGGEST people I have ever seen. Many of these guys were six foot three or four, very broad and very powerfully built, wearing loose cotton robes. Happily, few people carried weapons on the streets. My days there were spent eating boring cheap food, mostly beans ("ful") and coarse bread, walking around until it got TOO hot, and then sitting somewhere debilitated until the evening breeze brought life back to the city.

## Grief at the American Club

Motivated by the enervating midday heat, I inquired if Khartoum had anything resembling a municipal swimming pool. That seemed to be a concept a little bit too progressive for that hot, dusty African city, but I heard that there was a swimming pool at "the American Club". Getting approximate directions to the place, I walked that direction the next day about 10 am. I did manage to find it, on a dusty, broken up, partially paved street, with a bored Sudanese man sitting in a sentry box beside the gate. I asked if I could come in to have a swim, and showed him my US passport. Nope, but I could get a "guest membership" for only $50 USD. Ouch, my vagabonding budget was $50 per week for transport, food, lodging, entertainment, film, everything, so that was considerably too steep. I chatted with the gateman, buttered him up, gave him cigarettes, (no, I don't smoke, but always carried cigarettes for gifts) but he had heard it all before, and I failed to get in for a free swim. No "silver tongue" this time.

Disappointed and discouraged, I walked back towards the center of town. By that time it was really hot, and walking was a pain, through pounding sun with squinted eyes, all dusty colors everywhere limited to dun, gray, and brown. After half a mile I saw a vision. There, across the littered street, between the huge robed black men, nearly lost in the heat shimmer, was a spot of blue and gold. As it approached me it slowly separated from the glare and resolved itself into a young blond woman wearing a pale blue cotton summer dress. Usually I do NOT think quickly, but in this one instance, I did not miss the opportunity. I crossed the street, confronted the pretty vision, and said in English, "Please excuse me, I'm trying to find the American Club, do you know where it is?" A hit. She happened to be going there, and would show me the way! Turned out to be a 17 year old Californian gal who we will call Lucy. Her father was an American oil company international troubleshooter, and had been transferred to Khartoum for six months. Lucy had already been in the Sudan for three of those months and was BORED OUT OF HER MIND. For me this was a good situation.

When we reached the American Club together, I was relieved that my buddy the gateman did not say anything to give me away, though he did give me serious stink-eye. Lucy invited me in for a swim as a guest on her membership, and everything seemed to be going along quite well. There were a dozen white folks lounging around a small swimming pool, and she introduced me to several, including a few short fit young men with suspiciously short haircuts. The cool water was wonderful, almost a new experience, and sharing it with a pretty gal in a brief swimsuit made it all even better. Then, lying on a borrowed towel beside the pool, things went rapidly to Hades. The short-haired, fit young men came over to sit close to us, and proceeded to harry, annoy, and harass us. They were, of course, part of the local US Marine Corps consulate guard, and they took immediate and serious dislike to my shabby clothing and long hair. Lucy was on a first name basis with them, but clearly was siding with me in the verbal conflict which was heating up. I was winning the war of wits, but it wasn't making any impression on them. These guys were determined to start a fight with me. They really REALLY wanted any excuse to pound me senseless, to demonstrate their testosterone-poisoned superiority. They insulted me, they insulted Lucy, and were generally aggressive and obnoxious. Finally we reached the point where they were deliberately nudging and pushing me, trying to get me to take a swing at one of them. Now, mind you, I am not that big a fool. I know they train all of those quarter-wit little banty Marines to kill with their bare hands. Therefore I spent a very unpleasant hour swallowing their gibes.

It seemed strange and paradoxical to me that there in Africa, all of the local people were being very friendly to me, while my own countrymen of my own age were posing a very real and immediate danger. I figured that I understood what was going on in their underdeveloped minds, and to some extent I sympathized. I imagined that they had all been "bird dogging" Lucy for three months with no apparent success, and unexpectedly a new beau shows up on the scene, with what appeared to be a much closer relationship than they had achieved. As you can imagine, pretty, unmarried white women were an extremely rare quantity in Khartoum. That would have been plenty of reason to hate me, even without considering the lightning-rod-effect of my shoulder-length brown hair. Lucy and I finally left together, I walked her home and was introduced to her parents. They viewed me with undisguised and abiding distrust. Fair enough. For the next few days Lucy and I spent most of each day together, even going back to the swimming pool once, to be hassled by a different set of Marines. There was nothing naughty going on between us, mind you, I was a paragon of gentlemanly behavior the whole time I escorted my innocent little girlfriend.

# City Girl

Strolling beside the Nile, under the fragrant flowering trees, late at night, I discovered that Lucy was the quintessential city girl. I was pointing out some of the constellations to her, and explaining them in true astronomy-nerd fashion. I remarked that the pole star was out of sight this far south, but that all of the stars rotate around it. Lucy said, amazed by a new idea, "Do the stars move?" Yes, America is a really wonderful place!! You can grow to be 17 years old and still be completely insulated from nature and the real world.

I ended our little tryst by inviting Lucy to accompany me to the wilds of southern Sudan and back to Khartoum, and she thought that would be a wonderful idea. Of course, her folks put the kibosh on that plan, and I don't blame them one bit. A few weeks later I was quite grateful that she hadn't come along, as I found that just taking care of myself was plenty to worry about, without a cute little dependent to protect. (Flash forward) I did write to Lucy sporadically from various exotic ports. Four years later, having completed my vagabond's world-tour, I tracked down Lucy in California, and she drove down from her university to stay with me for a long weekend. I then got to hear the other side of the story. Seems that the Khartoum Marines had been sniffing around her just as I suspected, but with unimagined success. Prior to my arrival Lucy had been taking three or four of them to bed in rotation and my presence was cutting them out!!! The clever little woman had organized her own personal stud farm. NO WONDER the random vagabond freak was cordially despised by the Khartoum contingent of U.S. Marines!!

I did see some interesting things at the bleak youth hostel. There on Thursday night I was treated to the best display of belly dancing I have ever witnessed. Unfortunately, it was many male Egyptian students belly dancing for other male Egyptian students. They were really quite good at it, and the loud, scratchy recorded music was wild and wanton. I wasn't shocked, already being acquainted with the fact that many (most?) Arab men are bi-sexual, and being denied any access to their own women when young, they take romance where they can find it.

## Holy Herd

The guy who manned the gate at the youth hostel was a nice Dinka tribal, bright and always cheerful, speaking tolerable English. His Christian name was Kenneth. The Canadian couple had brought with them on their African tour a thin book of photographs titled "Canada in Pictures". I had looked through the photos, and there was one in there that I suspected might have a dramatic effect on Kenneth. Therefore I watched him intently, without seeming to do so, as he looked at the pictures. I was correct. He turned a page, and SLAMMED the book shut, wild eyed! He opened it again, and slammed it shut again! Then he very slowly opened the book a third time, and began to count, his eyes wide with amazement and longing. The picture was of a huge herd of Canadian cattle, photographed from the air. To the Dinka, cattle are both ultimate wealth and holy religious objects. I'm sure Kenneth had a religious satori right there sitting on his stool at the youth hostel gate. He carefully counted every one of the thousands of cattle in the photograph. His eyes were all misty when he finished.

## The Train to Wau

Having exhausted the historical, cultural, and culinary attractions of Khartoum, I decided that I would ride the Nile steamer north with the flow of current from Juba in far southern Sudan. It then only remained to discover how I would get to Juba overland. Having assiduously collected information from northbound vagabonds whom I had met, the most likely route seemed to be the Sudanese railway 900 miles out through the middle of nowhere to a dot on the map called Wau. Then trust to luck to find some random transport from Wau over another 500 miles of unimproved dirt tracks to Juba. Yes, the Sudan is BIG ! To look at it on the map it really doesn't impress, but Sudan is actually larger than all of Western Europe combined! The train to Wau originated at Khartoum and ran only twice a week. The railway ended short at Wau due to the fact that the British had not completed the line any farther than Wau when Sudan achieved independence 20 years previously. Not coincidentally, Wau was still the terminus.

Vagabond rumors indicated that the Wau train could be extremely crowded. In advance, therefore, I bought myself a ticket to Wau, fourth class with student discount for about $6, and also shopped the native market for lots of dried dates and other non-perishable food. Two hours before the train was due to depart Khartoum I was on the platform with my pack, ready to fight for a fourth-class bench seat. There were lots of city Sudanese on the platform with me, all having exactly the same intention; excitement was high, and tension crackled through the crowd. About 300 yards away, along a curving track, we could see a huge shed with smoke coming out of it. We all expected the train to issue from the darkness inside, arriving with a flourish at the platform in front of us, at which point we would all vigorously scramble into the welcoming carriages, staking out our personal territories. Well, we had imagined

MOST of that correctly. When the train did finally emerge into the sunlight, 90 minutes after it was scheduled to depart, and moved ponderously towards us, a strange, whispering sigh, almost a low groan, rippled through the platform crowd. The entire train was already BLACK with humanity, people hanging out of every window, and completely covering the roofs of every carriage!! Since the train only ran twice a week, those Sudanese in the know had already been living in the carriages for a day or two! Ouch, I was late again.

OK, by then I was familiar with Sudanese train-riding etiquette. I quickly clambered up onto the crowded roof of a carriage about two-thirds of the way back, forcefully wedged my pack down between the narrow butts of two wild-looking tribal gentlemen, and sat on it. I offered each of them a hard lemon candy and a cigarette in the hopes that they would not challenge my right to squat there. Their tribal facial scars crinkled as they smiled graciously, and I had a seat!

My Seat on the Train
Bulgarian Film meets
Kenyan Development

In return they offered me a taste of slippery home-brewed alcoholic beverage, which I tried, and a chew of tarry-looking tobacco, which I politely declined. A few hours later, a coal burning loco and tender, followed by 15 ancient passenger carriages, carrying well over two thousand human souls chugged majestically out of Khartoum, headed deep into central Africa. We followed the east bank of the Blue Nile south for about 100 miles. The sun, heat, and humidity were intense there in the narrow cultivated strip along the river. In late evening the locomotive turned its nose into the setting sun and rolled steadily across trestles over both the Blue and White Niles, and out into the deserts of southern Sudan.

A note about the geography and climate of southern Sudan is here appropriate. The scenery is very flat and featureless along the rail to Wau, excepting the numerous termite mounds. We started out moving through scrubby desert, which slowly changed over the miles into bushy desert, then into scrubby forest, and finally through patches of dense but cheerless dry forest. The train stopped often, at every little shabby-three-grass-huts-village, and there was always an unconscionably long delay before we started to move again. I soon realized that the train crew were scheduling things to maximize overtime pay, and I am sure that they were successful. According to the official schedule, we should have been seventy-one hours in transit to Wau. In fact we arrived ninety-six hours after our departure. You can do the math. The average speed of the journey was about nine miles per hour.

Ninety six hours is a long time to sit on the roof of a railway carriage, especially a crowded one. Lots of folks finished their journey along the route, and lots more joined up along the way, so the density of the throng varied over time. When leaving Khartoum we were so crowded that I could only get a place to sit a few feet down from the ridge of the carriage roof. This position had some distinct disadvantages. Firstly, since many Sudanese are addicted to tobacco chewing, spitting is almost continuous. Secondly, such a seat became rather sporting when folks up-roof shifted their positions, at times threatening to slide me off over the rounded edges. Fortunately, I was bigger and stronger than the average southern Sudanese man, so by digging in with my heels, and the heels of my hands, I could maintain my position, in spite of down-roof pressure. After the roof crowd thinned, I claimed a ridge seat, which I never afterward relinquished. Several travelers did fall off the roof during the journey. I could tell when someone had fallen off, because the train would stop, and then back up for a mile or two. Two of those falling off were killed in the process, the others being only injured. My local informants said this casualty level from falling was about average for a trip to Wau.

My fellow travelers on the train to Wau were quite picturesque. An unwritten rule seemed to be 'men only' on the roof, so all of the women and children were inside the carriages. There were several versions of the "typical" man's costume, ranging from simple cheesecloth boxer shorts, through short sleeved cheesecloth shifts, a few unarmed soldiers in khaki going home on leave, and finally including glorious traditional tribal costumes. The farther south we progressed, the higher the proportion of tribal passengers became, and the wilder and more amazing became the appearance of these local people. After leaving the Nile, many of the gents on the roof at any given time were armed, carrying 2 to 6 evil-looking iron-tipped javelins in one hand, as well as an ax or fighting stick in the other. The socketed blades of these short lances were about 18" long, leaf shaped, and no wider than an inch. The shafts were only about 3/4" thick at maximum so one hand could comfortably grasp a number of them. Deadly looking, they were. It seems the Sudanese carry multiples so that they can afford to throw a few, and still not find themselves unarmed. All of the iron work was locally done, and each spear-point was hand made. The four-foot-long fighting sticks were made out of ironwood, which is extremely well named, very dense, hard, heavy and unsympathetic pieces of equipment. The axes were unspectacular small-bladed affairs. Strangely, none of the weapons were ornamented in any way. They gave the message that they were 'all business'. Looking along the roof of the train, I had the impression of a long, thin porcupine, each sitting man holding his bundle of spears erect.

Sudanese tribals in the south are easily the most interesting and colorful of any group of unsophisticated people I have ever encountered. The major tribal areas through which the train passed were the Nuer, the Shilluk, and the Dinka, (your spellings may differ). Sudan is the place where earlobe stretching has passed all reasonable belief. I saw one guy who had decorated himself with a yellow quart oil can through each earlobe! Another more practical man had his sleeping mat rolled up and held behind his head by an earlobe looped over either end. The Dinka wear more jewelry per-capita than anyone else on earth. A well-dressed Dinka man or woman has many toe rings, followed by ankle bracelets, below knee bracelets, above knee bracelets, a large elaborate beaded girdle, many necklaces, above elbow bracelets, below elbow bracelets, wrist bracelets, and plenty of finger rings, in addition to beaded collars and pectorals, and up to 15 earrings in each ear !! Most of the tribes have distinctive patterns of facial and body scars as a rite of passage into manhood. Top all that off with a beaded tiara or helmet, some feathers, and an occasional pair of dark sunglasses, and you can imagine that they are something to behold!!

## Communards

When the trip was truly launched, and a routine had been established, an informal local commune sprang up on my section of carriage roof. Soon about 20 of us were cooperating, and sharing food, my dried dates being particularly well received every time they came out of the backpack. Although I did not have a single word of any language in common with any of my neighbors, I was casually accepted as one of the guys. When climbing back up to our perch, I would hold the weapons of those ahead of me, and pass them up to the owners, and they would in turn wait for me, and give me a hand-up. Also, when some would climb down from the carriage at a stop, others would protect the common luggage, and we made certain that all of the communards still had a good place to sit when the train moved forward once more. I commented thankfully to myself how wonderful it was that all of these men of various tribes were really so peaceful, and so easy to get along with, because they looked SO fierce and heavily-armed and dangerous. Once our commune gelled, life was OK up there on the railway carriage roof.

The daily routine was actually pretty deadening. I would sit baking on the roof looking at the boring scenery passing by, and when we stopped at a village of grass huts, I would climb down to try to refill my 2-liter water bottle, and to stretch my legs and visit a little bit. In visiting, I met a few Sudanese passengers who spoke some English.

## *Staying Hydrated*

The water replenishment wasn't too difficult, because when the local boys heard the train approaching their village, some would run to the nearest buffalo wallow, dip up a plastic pail of horrible greasy gray water, and run to the train to sell it for a piaster per fill-up. Other times there was a mud hole not too far from the tracks. Really wasn't too good a situation. Often only a 2" depth of this water was completely opaque, and it tasted bad, to boot, but that was all that was available. It was quite hot up on the roof in the hammering sun, and I spent some of the time being darn thirsty. I did use aqueous iodine to disinfect the water, but sometimes it was not quite possible to wait the whole half hour after treating the water before drinking. I had made up my mind before I left the U.S. that I would spend a LOT of the time on the road being sick, so that I wouldn't be surprised when it happened, but at that point my health was still holding out.

Yes, I Drank this Water, in Spite of Cow Excrement, No Other Choice

## Curious Bushman

At one of the frequent stops, I met a Bushman at the water hole !!! I have NO idea why he had wandered so far north, but there was no question of his identity. The local blacks were very curious about him as well, and considered him a feature. We 'conversed' for a time, he examined my equipment, and I his. His face was open and friendly, and his skin was a pleasing rusty-ocher color, much lighter than the very black skin of all those living in that part of the world. He was carrying well-worn home-made leather sandals and also a little bow and arrows, the only examples of either I ever saw in use in Africa. When he allowed me to open his quiver of nasty little barbed arrows, I asked him using sign language if they were poisoned. The locals laughed at my pantomime of dying from poison. My bushman buddy assured me that his arrows were not poisoned.

## First Farangi

I have no doubt that I was the first white skinned person some of the children along the way had ever seen. I imagine that Farangi vagabonds ride the train in one direction or the other every month, but even in villages within walking distance of the railway, white skins would have been extremely uncommon. Several times small groups of children, up to about 7 years old, screamed and pointed and hid behind their parents when they spotted me. The parents, on one occasion, obviously understanding the ways of white travelers, waved at me, correctly assuming that I would wave back. This display caused their little ones to scream and hide again, which gave the elders a good laugh.

The Train to Wau
Bulgarian Film meets
Kenyan Development

## Primal Man

At one point on the journey, after I had been, in some mysterious fashion, judged worthy, I was granted a short glimpse of Primal Man himself. Yep, there he was, standing on top of a termite mound, gravely watching the train pass by. He stood proudly, completely naked except for a thick uniform coating of gray dust, no adornments, holding in his left hand a short, crude club. I was thrilled to have been permitted to burn his image into my retina. I will never forget it.

After riding for more than a day, I began to suspect that the train ride on the roof was free, because nobody had demanded a ticket. Late the second day, however, while the train rattled along, the ticket collectors came along the roof for the first time. They were two enormous men wearing Arab robes, and they were punching everybody's tickets, stepping carefully over the passengers and working their way towards the engine. The guy with the ticket punch had a big naked knife in his other hand, and his companion had a cocked 38 caliber single action revolver in his fist and a huge knife in his belt!!! Nobody was giving them ANY trouble, but they looked pretty nervous, their eyes darting around to try to keep as many of my neighbors in view as possible. Yow, that forced me to reconsider my judgment of the nice, peaceful, friendly folks crowded all around me on the roof. If the ticket collectors had to go armed to the teeth, maybe, - - - - - just maybe, - - my fellow communards were not always as peaceable and easy to get along with as I had concluded.

That night I woke about midnight, sleeping wedged between two of my wild companions, my forehead jammed against the shoulder of a particularly smelly gent. We were stopped, which was not unusual, but I could just make out the short smokestack of the locomotive against the horizon, and it was not smoking. The fires had been banked. That had never happened before. I climbed down from the roof to make a necessary hydraulic adjustment, and found that the ground on both sides of the train was covered with people who had climbed out of the packed carriages, and were sleeping there. I stepped over folks in the darkness until I got to the edge of the inhabited area and took care of my errand. On my way back to the train, one of my English-speaking acquaintances, a soldier going home on furlough, popped up and greeted me quietly. "Hello, mister Chih-kuh." "Hello, mister Adam. How long do we stop here?" He informed me that we were waiting for sunrise to go through the next big patch of scrubby forest. When I quizzed him as to why, he answered in a refreshingly concise and ingenuous manner. "We are afraid." whispered Adam. "What makes you afraid?" I watched as he carefully formulated his reply, translating it in his head. "Wild animals and wild people" was the memorable reply.

Treeless Village

## Wild Animals and Wild People

When mister Adam told me that the threat of "Wild animals and wild people" was keeping the train to Wau parked in the middle of nowhere until daylight, I immediately thought to myself 'You guys are really chicken-hearted, c'mon, let's go on down the track to Wau where I may be able to find a shower!', but I didn't say anything at all, keeping my opinions to myself. I lay down on the ground, wrapped up my head in my Al Fatah towel, and went back to sleep.

Finally the sun oozed above the dusty trees to the east. The railway crew diddled about for another half hour, and we continued south, through the forest with the dangerous reputation. This third day's journey was much like the previous two, moving through flat landscape, mostly dry thickets made up of individually thin but densely packed trees. As before, we stopped at every desolate grass hut village, and as before, my focus was on trying to stay comfortable and hydrated.

## Self Congratulation begins
## a Bit Too Early

Just before noon we stopped at a small nameless village in a good-sized clearing. I was maneuvering into position to refill my water bottle when I heard a commotion at some distance, and moved to a point where I could see what was going on. There at the far edge of the clearing, about 200 yards away, I could see seven men just KILLING two soldiers who were already lying on the ground. The wild-looking attackers each had an ironwood fighting stick, standing in a circle around the two inert forms pounding them **WHACKWHACKWHACKWHACK** with all of their might! They were putting so much power into the blows that it seemed their feet were lifting off the ground with each strike!! Yowee!! Two of my fellow communards took their identical fighting clubs and ran to the rescue. I grabbed an unsatisfactory piece of firewood and ran in the same direction.

Fortunately, by the time I arrived, the fight was over. The seven original assailants, seeing about 30 people running to the rescue, only waited for the first few to arrive, did a little face-saving stick-fighting, and then ran into the bushes, chased by three of the most stalwart from the train. So, there we were, the proud group of rescuers standing around at the edge of the forest, with everyone talking fast. Dinka and English and Shilluk and Nuer and Swahili could all be heard, but it all had exactly the same tone. Everyone was telling each other the same thing - "Ain't we COOL !?!   Did you see those suckers RUN from us ?!? Man, we really showed those guys, didn't we !!"

Soldiers arrived from the train out of breath and began to blanket-carry their two unconscious comrades back towards the rails. I ditched my firewood and watched them. But, there was something strange going on back at the distant train, now that I looked at it. - - - - Yep, no question about it, the folks on the roof were getting down from there, and there was nothing calm about it, they were coming down **IN A HURRY** and PACKING themselves bodily into the already jammed carriages. The big heavy wooden shutters were dropping down "Clump, Clump, Clumpclumpclump, Clump" sealing the windows.

Now I figured from up there they could probably see something that I couldn't see from where I was. So I started walking casually, back in the direction of the train, - gotta maintain cool. Just about that time the three passengers who had chased the bad guys into the forest zoomed past me **RUNNING FLAT OUT** for the train, looking back over their shoulders with their eyes bugging out!!! Well, I assure you that it is very easy to get sucked along in a situation like that, and I was moving at my best speed before I ever looked back. Sure enough, the local wild men hadn't run too far back into the forest, they had only gone back to their huts to get their spears, and now they were back chasing us toward the railway!! And those guys were not fooling around, they were spearing people!

At that point, running hard for the train, I was feeling awfully conspicuous. I was slower than the running Sudanese, I had much broader shoulders, and with everyone else in sight wearing either khaki or black skin, I had on a yellow T-shirt !!! I MUST have been the greatest target available, but I don't think any of the nasty javelins were aimed at me personally, because none landed close. I made it to the train un-speared!! But there was still a problem. There were SO many people now packed into the carriages that no more could fit inside, and the only room available was on the bottom step at the end of a carriage, facing outward with my back against a solid mass of humanity, watching the locals run up and throw their lances at the train!! It was completely amazing, and I could hardly believe my eyes! Inside my head I was shouting - "This isn't 1975, it could be 100 years ago!"

The word got up to the engine, and we pulled chuggingly away. At that point the spear-chuckers started jumping around wildly, waving their remaining javelins over their heads, and chanting joyously. And I could tell from the familiar tone exactly what they were saying. Of course it was - "Did you SEE all those boys RUN from us ? ! ? We REALLY scared those buggers ! ! ! They'll learn not to mess with US, won't they ! ? !" I am pretty sure that we did not leave anyone behind when we departed, but I cannot begin to imagine how much worse the situation would have been if the same scene had been enacted in the darkness. I now understood why we had waited until daylight to pass through that region. I silently apologized to those controlling the movements of the train for ever believing they were chicken-hearted.

## Six Ampoules

We rode for about a half hour and then stopped again, and everyone was busy getting sorted out, back up onto the roofs, and finding their belongings. During this confusing time mister Adam appeared at my elbow, saying " Men are hurt, mister Chih-Kuh, and you must come to see them." I didn't know what he was talking about, but accompanied him a few carriages forward to where the casualties were being collected. That was when I discovered that out of 2000 people on the train, my white skin and tiny 1" by 1" by 3" first aid kit made me the best we could do for a doctor!! Well, alright then, I went back to my Boy Scout and hospital-orderly training, and began administering as best I could. I found six little glass ampoules in the kit, four red-brown and two white. The red-brown ones proved to be Mercurochrome, and I broke them open one by one and used them to treat spear damage, happily all flesh-wounds.

We were remarkably lucky in that none of the injured had been speared into the body cavity, which is THE most likely injury. A guy had been speared in the butt, and another had been badly cut on his shoulder by a very near miss. One poor guy had taken a javelin in the front of his shin, and the point was in the bone so solidly that I could not pull it out, even standing over him using my powerful leg muscles as others anchored his leg. So I disinfected it as best I could and wrapped a little gauze around the entry point. Using dabs of antiseptic creme and band-aids I treated a couple of contusions from the stick fight.

Then Adam took me up into one of the carriages where the two badly-beaten guys were lying. Those two were still mostly senseless, and one of them had been hit so hard in the back of his head that his nose had bled profusely. From my two summers spent as an emergency-room orderly I knew that to be a very bad sign. What could I do for them? Not much, Ok, put their feet up higher than their heads to treat them for shock, but that seemed pretty unsatisfactory. Then I discovered that my two little white ampoules were smelling salts, exactly what I needed in my three cubic inch first aid kit! I broke one open, and held it under the noses in turn, and they both sputtered and snapped their faces away, then snorting groggily awake. I left solemn instructions, through Adam's translation, that the nose-bleeder's friends were NOT UNDER ANY CIRCUMSTANCES to allow him to go to sleep until we reached the doctor at Wau. I was very much afraid that if he went to sleep, he would slip into a coma, and die before we could do anything else. Also, I knew that in some cultures, if you treat an injured person, you become responsible for his fate. Apparently I was lucky, and keeping him awake worked, because everyone was still alive a day and a half later when we reached Wau. Well, everyone, that is, if we do not count the two men who were killed by falling off, but those were not my responsibility.

## Wau as a Tourist Destination

The final destination of the train to Wau was reached without further major excitement. Wau is not very big, and had no hotel. I found a guest house with four windowless rooms for the use of government employees who might be sent there. Being windowless wasn't a big problem, because the rooms were open under the eaves to the outside world. I bought more mosquito coils from a shop. I bargained for a room for the night ($2), and had a truly wonderful shower, my first in more than 4 days. It was heavenly, and my pleasure in it was only diluted by the fact that I had to keep the water strictly out of my mouth, nose, eyes, and ears. Lots of nasty little parasites in the local water, according to my best information. If you happen to get them inside you they eventually make you go blind, and do even worse things to your innards. The guest house room did have a string bed, however, which felt extremely nice and comfortable, as it was the first time I had slept anywhere but on the hard ground or train roof since leaving Aswan more than three weeks previously. - - - Luxury. - - - The room even had a bare electric light bulb hanging from the rafters!

There were said to be a couple of missions with clinics on the outskirts of town, but I never saw them. I did spot a couple of white folks at a distance in my daily wanderings around town. I don't remember a single paved road in the hot, humid overgrown village. Garbage was pretty much everywhere, and flocks of HUGE turkey vultures scavenged in the streets themselves, walking about proudly, ignored by the human inhabitants. I soon went looking for transport to Juba, 500 miles farther south over unimproved tracks. I talked to every building which had a truck parked outside, and queried everyone who greeted me in English or French, but in truth there was nothing headed south. Oh, well, I needed a few days rest anyway. So, with no transport south available it remained for me to amuse myself.

This wasn't too difficult.

## Disturbing Foods

A good-sized native market was in progress at the edge of town every day, and I wandered it often. I saw one man sitting on the ground next to a large stack of big roasted termites. Hmmmm - this reminded me that when I began my vagabond's tour, I had vowed to myself that I would eat everything I found the local people eating. I asked the termite vendor using sign language if his bugs were to eat. He agreed that this was the reason they were for sale. A small attentive crowd gathered to observe. I chose two of the biggest termites and began to bargain. After awhile we agreed on a tiny price for two termites. I took them, and handed him one back saying "OK, you eat it now." Everybody laughed. He ate his, and, now assured that I was not being set up for a good joke, I ate mine. It was crunchy, not much taste to it. I had no burning desire to eat more roasted termites, but at least I had kept my vow. (Historical footnote - the first country in which I spent any time on my vagabond's tour had been Italy, in which I found the local people eating two different foods which I just could NOT force myself to sample, each being infinitely more horrible than roasted termites, but that is another story. Thus I almost immediately broke my vow, but always kept it afterward in all countries EXCEPT Italy.)

There was one cafe in Wau town, called "Unity Garden". It was a few battered, flimsy folding chairs and tables set outdoors in a dusty little square and lit by strings of colored Christmas lights. In one corner was a double statue, gaudily painted, showing a handsome, robed Arab-looking northern Sudanese offering his hand in friendship to a bulging-eyed, grinning, cartoonish black southern Sudanese in a blue T shirt and bright red shorts. Unity Garden was created by the government to unambiguously demonstrate the fact that the ruling northern Arab Sudanese had recently militarily defeated the rebellious southern Christian/Animist Sudanese. I found out later that there was another "Unity Garden" in Juba. The menu consisted of ful (beans), coarse bread, tea, and sometimes fried eggs and mystery-meat kabobs. There was also a soggy, sticky pasta dish with bright pink sauce euphemistically referred to as "'spaghetti". I ate there every night of my six in Wau because they also had two electric table fans, and a tatty record player with a scratchy LP by Crosby Stills and Nash, which they played over and over again. It had, you see, been a long time since I had heard any western music.

Magic
Traveling
Bangle

Gin and Tonic in an
Enameled Cup

Wau's Market

# Mister Bojo

There was one building in town containing a generator-powered ice machine. On my second day in Wau I was standing next to a blacksmith's shop, which was really just a series of little reed awnings over a couple of hole-in-the-ground forges all strung along an outside wall, with about a dozen folks working there. The southern Sudanese can make ANYTHING out of metal. They were in process of cutting a truck frame into pieces using only the charcoal-fueled forge and a cold chisel. They heated a section of the frame glowing cherry red hot, then hit it there with a sledge-hammered cold chisel a few times, then repeated the process. They cut it completely in two in only six iterations! Others in the shop were cutting shapes out of sheet metal petrol tins and bending them to make watering cans, or steerable toy trucks, or all sorts of other things out of them using big soldering irons. I was fascinated.

After a while, an older man, apparently the owner of the blacksmith shop, came bustling up to me officiously, and in a rude and peremptory fashion handed me a small metal bowl, and told me in English to go to the ice store and bring him back some ice water. He then immediately turned away. I could tell that this was some kind of a test, but had no idea what the rules were. So, I walked calmly away, over to the ice store on the other side of town, asked them to fill the bowl with cool water, and brought it back to the blacksmith about 20 minutes later. He seemed pretty surprised to see me back with his water, smiled in an ambiguous fashion, and immediately made me a comfortable place to sit on the ground in his shop, with my back to the wall. To this day I am not sure if I passed the friendship test, or if he had deliberately sent me on a "woman's errand", fetching water, which no real man would agree to perform, and I had therefore failed SO horribly that he was embarrassed into being nice to me. From that moment on "Mister Bojo" and I were good friends, and I spent part of each day sitting in the blacksmith's shop, checking out the amazing craftsmanship that these clever men performed with the simplest of tools. I gave Mister Bojo a pack of good English Player cigarettes, and the next day he gave me a spear-point, identical to the ones I had seen put to excellent use on the train ride several days previously. I have that spear-point here now, so many years later, beside my keyboard as I write.

Gift from
Mister Bojo

# By Truck to Juba

I finally heard about a truck that was leaving to the south in a few days, and bargained with the owners for a ride all the way to Juba. We reached agreement, and two mornings later I was part of a small throng of Sudanese standing around a stake bed truck, while the four-man truck crew loaded lots of luggage in an even layer at the bottom of the 10' by 22' bed. Being a curiosity, I was allowed to board first, and sat on my pack with my back against the cab. Then everyone else boarded. It was pretty crowded, as with most transport in the Sudan. Lots of men, women, and children, all going south for any of a number of reasons. We soon began to motor south, the group in high spirits. This truck served the functions of both bus and shipping line. It was owned by the operators and had no fixed schedule, going where profit dictated. Since there were plenty of folks waiting in Wau for transport south, that is where it was decided the truck would go.

The truck crew were very strict in enforcing their rule about how many people could board the truck along the way. The only rule was "You have to pay to get on". Therefore the standard boarding scenario went like this. The crowded truck approaches an enormous 300 pound woman sitting on two huge burlap bags of peanuts beside the track. Everyone in the back of the truck grimaces as the truck stops for her, and bargaining for a ride takes place. Now, the truck is already COMPLETELY full with people jammed together in the back, so how is the new material loaded? Quite easily. The truck crew actually pair up to (one, two, thREE !) throw the massive bags of peanuts up over the stake rails on top of the passengers, who then, naturally, squirm out from underneath, and the peanuts are loaded !! Then the huge woman climbs up the outside of the stakes and perches precariously at the top above us for a few horrible seconds, while those passengers below her cringe. She launches herself butt-first into the scrum, landing crushingly on a half dozen folks, who, again, squirm out from under her, and, she has a place to sit!! Worked very well in retrospect. At one point the truck was so crowded that I decided to count how many folks were riding in the back. I counted 75, which was SO high that I knew I had somehow blown the counting, and counted again. My second passenger count came up 77.

View from My Seat on the Truck
( Bulgarian Film meets Kenyan Development )

The truck ride went on for three days and three nights. Most of the time there was a discernible unimproved road, and the drivers were extremely good at choosing a path through the multiple sets of corrugations and ruts with minimum jolting. Some of the time we were just driving along dry stream-beds. We usually stopped for the night at a little village or a lonely trade store, whereupon everyone would get down, fix themselves some food, and curl up on the ground to sleep. Eight of the other passengers turned out to be a traveling performing troupe, on a mission from the Sudanese government to put on shows of acrobatics/tumbling/boxing/bed-of-nails lying/flaming hoop jumping/guitar playing at various far flung villages. They were headed from Wau to a town called Maridi, deep in the southern jungle. Seemed a very strange mission to me, but these young men were quite friendly to me, and I was grateful that they made room for me on their big tumbling mats at night, which was much better than sleeping on the ground. They also "translated" for me, even though none of them spoke English or French. They were rather modern gents, wearing European-style clothing, with two of them even having processed straightened hair.

## Green Mangos, mostly

So, with the dearth of shops in that part of the world, what did I eat? Unripe mangoes, mostly. For most of two days we drove through HUGE forests of mango trees. From time to time the truck would stop, and everyone would get down and throw things up into the trees to knock down the not-quite-ripe fruit. I ate lots of green mangoes, and so did everyone else. Things got pretty sticky. I couldn't look a mango in the face for a couple of years after that trip, having gotten completely sick of them. After one stop, as we drove away, I felt something going on in the crowd behind me. Twisting around, I found a little kid calmly wiping his sticky hands on my shirt. He wasn't embarrassed about this at all, and his mother seemed puzzled that I would object to this perfectly logical use of my clothing.

Another time I had moved a little way off from the truck to throw rocks into the trees, and was surprised when something whacked me hard across my head and shoulders from behind! Spinning around and backing up quickly, I found a wizened little old man with a big leafy branch maneuvering for another whack at me and cussing me out vituperously in some local dialect!! Some of the acrobats came and got between him and me, and talked him into calming down. Hundreds of thousands of wild mango trees all around, but according to my assailant, I had been messing about with one of HIS own personal mango trees!! I guess he found it necessary to deal firmly with all those dirty mango thieves masquerading as Farangi vagabonds. The third and last night of the journey I heard a disturbing loud roaring at some distance away. I had still not seen any big wild animals in Africa, though I had been watching for them. All I had seen were some baboons and lots of huge storks and vultures. In the morning I found out from the acrobats that I had heard a hippo roaring!  I redoubled my big-animal-spotting efforts after that.

The truck ride from Wau to Juba eventually entered real, serious forests in the far south of the country, with beautiful big trees. The entertaining troupe finished their journey at Maridi, a lovely clean village. Most of Maridi snuggled in under the most enormous single tree I have ever seen. Much later that day we reached the river which is a tributary to the White Nile, and I got a look at Juba.

## Welcome to Juba

There was really not much to see there. Juba is on an open plain with scattered stands of trees on the west bank of the brown river, and was big enough to have both an airfield and a hotel. There was also a rundown building marked "Tourist Center", but it was eternally closed. The faded red and white painted sign sat in a filthy rubbished yard, wrapped in multiple strands of rusting barbed wire. It was all so attractive and welcoming that I took a photo of the place.

Juba's "Hotel Africa" was pretty basic, but still nice. It was essentially a big mosquito-screened porch having lots of steel bedsteads with thin mattresses scattered around the concrete floor. There were a few private rooms, but I signed up for a bed in the completely visible dormitory area for $2 per night. I met two Dutch vagabonds there who were also waiting for the

Nile steamer. They were personable and unobjectionable, and they had a bag of marijuana. We chatted for a while, and then walked down to the Nile in the evening. The three of us sat with our legs hanging over the steep sloping bank of the brown river, languorously smoking dope as the red ball of the sun sank below the horizon. It was very peaceful and beautiful, and the mosquitoes were not yet out in force.

Tributary to the Nile

Very suddenly, without warning, a hippo surfaced about 15 feet away from us, blew bubbles out his nose, looked us over with its little piggy eyes, and just as quickly submerged again! Yowee, all three of us, wild-eyed, looked first to the others for reassurance that we all had seen the same thing, and that it had not been a THC-enabled hallucination! So I finally got to see a big African wild animal, but only for a few seconds. The Dinka actively hunt and eat the hippos, and it was said to be quite unusual to see one that near Juba.

## Dinka Dances

Every Friday night in a huge field beside the river there occurred big dances with all of the Dinka tribes in the surrounding area participating. The young men of each village form teams, from 6 to 25 strong, all dressed up in their best jewelry, with a common "theme" to the costumes of each contingent. One group might all be sporting kilts of cow's tails and carrying long, flexible branches, with a few leaves at the end. The next team might have leaves stuck in their headbands and each carry a short cudgel. The third perhaps gloried in armlets made of long, flopping cow tails, with strange, narrow gourds in every hand. The next might perhaps have strips of white cowhide hanging from neck collars all around, carrying battery flashlights held under their chins to make their features bottom-lit and terrifying. And each was different and distinct. I heard that in years past the Dinka used to all bring their spears to the dances, but since that custom resulted in casualties every week, the locals decided by popular acclaim to leave all real weapons home on Friday nights.

The first time I went to the dances I waited until after dark, and it was QUITE an experience. On the dark plain, in the still powerful, humid heat, between 500 and 1000 people milled about in the dusty dark to the staccato encouragement of throbbing drums. About two thirds of the crowd were Dinka spectators, with the remainder participating directly in the festivities. In the approximate center of the "dance" scrum was a single big log drum, with one sweating Dinka pounding either end forming two compelling, savage rhythms in counterpoint. The mass of people was not too claustrophobic or crowded, but there were people milling about in the dark and bumping into one another. Some Sudanese spectators walked around carrying hissing pump-gas lanterns, preternaturally bright, a few folks carried battery lamps, and several teams of "dancers" carried strange torches, burning smokily with an unearthly orange glow. Through this otherworldly throng, seen intermittently lit through clouds of dust, single file lines of the amazingly-attired dancers wound their way at random, chanting and stamping their feet in unison. From time to time the dancing lines would stop and in unison jump enthusiastically up and down in time with the drumbeats. Whenever I stopped moving to watch one contingent snake past, it was certain that shortly another group would unexpectedly issue from the crowded dusty darkness immediately behind me. For sure it was a magical place, supercharged with strange passion and a wild, palpable sexual tension. Transported by the compelling drumming, I flattered myself into believing I could feel the pulse of Africa itself.

A few days into my Juba sojourn another young Californian checked into the screen porch hotel. Paul was pretty laid back, and seemed a good, centered guy, so we bummed around town together. He had been in the Sudan for a month longer than I had, spending most of the additional time in the big oasis area of El Fasher, far to the west, about which place he was very enthusiastic. Paul also planned to experience the Nile steamer.

## *The Mean Drunk*

We Californians were sitting one afternoon drinking tea and writing at a rickety table in the dusty field next to Hotel Africa which doubled as a cafe. A tall, white-robed man who had arrived at the hotel recently (he had a private room) was sitting at a nearby table eyeing us malevolently. This gent had been drinking arak, solo, and his bottle was mostly empty. Not a good sign. He threw a few muttered English comments in our direction, so I invited him over to our table, bringing along his bottle and glass.

Conversation disclosed that "Mr. Adawa" considered himself a Sudanese government high official, but he wouldn't reveal much more than that to us. He was gruff and suspicious, and quite a disagreeable drunk. After several minutes of failed attempts to lure him into a friendly interaction, the self-important Sudanese government man had suffered enough. He leaned forward threateningly and said to Paul, in a slurred, gravelly voice,

"You think so you are clever man. But I say you are United State Central Intelligent Agent! I am Sudan government Security High Operation! When I say, in the prison you go!" We both chuckled, and replied, in effect, "Yeah-yeah-sure-sure, Mr. Very Important Adawa, why don't you just go inside and sleep it off?" Our casual attitude of disrespect drove the man into a sputtering rage !! He staggered to his feet and played his trump in a loud voice. "You say I am joke !!  I say to men follow you see every place, say to me every time scratch you ass !!"  Mr. Adawa then proceeded to spout a list of places Paul had been in the time he had been traveling around Sudan, IN DETAIL; where he slept, what he had eaten, to whom he had spoken, the information just came flooding out! I wasn't impressed until I glanced at Paul and saw that his face had gone tense, bloodless, and drawn. It became very obvious that everything the mean drunk was saying was accurate, and there was NO way he could have known those things unless he truly had people following Paul for the last couple of months!

Yowee !! Mr. Very Important Adawa was definitely no joke!

Paul therefore suddenly changed his plans from riding the Nile steamer to flying out of Sudan at the earliest possible moment!! He bought his air ticket the same afternoon, to Uganda two days hence. Now, why would anyone have to fly to Uganda which was only 200 miles south by road? Well, the Sudanese had a cute little scam going where foreigners could drive INTO Sudan along that road, but were forbidden to leave that way. I'm sure some Sudanese government officials had a big financial interest in Sudan Airways.

By this time, dysentery had established a secure presence in my guts. I was cramping and had the squirts pretty badly, doubtless due to ingesting some nasty little bacilli or amoeba. Having dysentery was pretty miserable, as it was my first experience with the disease, but certainly not my last. In unfortunate addition to the gut-gripes, I had developed some nasty 1" diameter tropical sores on the tops and sides of both of my feet. These were the result of voracious mosquitoes. I had successfully trained myself not to scratch the mosquito bites, at least not while awake. But while asleep, my heels unconsciously scratched the itching bites on the top of the opposite foot, and thus small wounds had been opened which had become septic, and grown into seeping open sores that just would not heal in that climate.

# Chick's Credo of Low-Budget Vagabonding

Happily I had convinced myself before I left home, that while vagabonding I would be sick OFTEN, so that I shouldn't be surprised when it happened. I contend that illness is all part of really experiencing the local culture. In Chick's credo of vagabonding, one must first genuinely internalize and accept the idea that he is NOBODY SPECIAL, but **Just Another Doofus**. The world made so much more sense to me once I truly understood this!

Then one travels to a new place, using the local transport,
interacts with the local people,
picks up 30 words of the local language,
inhabits the cheapest lodgings,
experiences the local ceremonies,
eats the local food,
samples the local diseases,
tries out the local intoxicants, and then
decides whether or not it is time to move on.
Well, it was about time to move on from Juba.

In theory the Nile steamer ran every week in each direction, from Juba to near Khartoum. In fact, since its route ran through the Sudd, the world's biggest, nastiest swamp, it tended to get stuck often, and ran rather less frequently than that. I arrived at Juba on the day before the steamer was scheduled to arrive. It actually arrived six days late. Oh, well, another typical demonstration of African time. The steamer itself was quite impressive. It was double decked, with a massive paddle-wheel at the rear (just visualize the Mississippi Belle with no frills). The upstairs had all of the tiny First Class cabins. The downstairs had some of the tinier Second Class cabins. On either side of this big, powered boat were strapped equally big un-powered double-decked barges. The cabins on these barges were the other 4/5ths of the second class cabins, and some rooms for the crew. Then, in front of each of these three large floating palaces were three additional double decked barges, these without any walls, and with a forest of steel poles and hundreds and hundreds of welded steel trays crammed together, making vertical "four decker" narrow bunks. All of these were the third class area !! So, all together, the Nile Steamer covered a piece of river almost twice the size of an American football field !! And it was crammed with about two thousand people on the deck class barges. The size and majesty of it took my breath away when I first saw it approaching from down-river, sounding its deep horn.

**Six-Hulled Nile Steamer**

( Bulgarian Film meets Kenyan Development )

Then, as it got close to the shore the odor of it reached me, and snatched my breath away again ! All of the third class deck area was one huge latrine. The unsophisticated Sudanese apparently realized that it was too much trouble to walk to the back barges and wait in line to use the toilet seats suspended above the open river, and had been shitting right on the decks between the bunks for the ten-day-long trip. Yipes !! The only saving grace was that most of the human excrement on the decks had been already desiccated by the heat, and was no longer stinking. Then I understood why the "vagabond telegraph" recommended claiming one of the TOP shelves of each four-level bunk set!

# Boarding the Nile Steamer

One side of the huge floating construct tied up at the riverbank, and four thin planks at four different points were balanced between the shore and the gunwale. People just came FLOWING off, carrying all sorts of stores and goods on their heads and shoulders. After a short while, this flow pattern was changed when folks started going back onto the steamer. This made for some interesting traffic jams on the narrow catwalks, with no rails, and folks trying to pass both directions simultaneously. I stood on the bank and watched until, after an hour, the traffic thinned. I balanced across the gangway, waded into the deep layer of garbage which covered the third class barges, picked out a top shelf, and climbed up there. I used a plastic ground cloth and a short length of rope to secure my claim on this spot. About then a minor steamer official appeared and informed me that I had to disembark. Nobody was allowed on the steamer until 3pm, about five hours hence because they needed to hose off the barges. Well, that was hard to disagree with. While we were talking, some of the kids who had been following me around managed to detach and steal my ground sheet and rope. Oh well.

I went back to the Hotel Africa to wait until boarding time. About 1 o'clock that afternoon I walked back down to the river to check out the steamer situation. BUMMER !! The whole place was already crawling with people !! Every bunk had already been claimed, and many hundreds of people were streaming on board the now-hosed barges carrying every imaginable load ! I was late again!! I dashed back to the screen porch, shouting for the Dutchmen! We all took our packs and rushed back down to the river to see if the situation could be salvaged. Not likely. We found some space on the upstairs of one of the barges and sat down on a piece of empty deck. We were soon informed that this deck was for "women only". Oh, well, OK, then.

We hustled down and then up another gangway and found a relatively open spot on that deck. Nope, "Soldiers only" on this deck. Well, I figured I could handle that. I found the highest ranking soldier I could and gave him cigarettes, tried to talk him into letting the three western freaks "enlist" for a short time. Nope, no good. I tried again, questioning why this whole deck could be set aside for soldiers only. He looked meaningfully at his Kalashnikov and wryly informed me, in decent English, that this was "the Law of Soldiers". I knew exactly what he meant. The first rule of overland vagabonding in Africa is "The man with the automatic weapon is always right". Shortly we found an empty place on one of the rear outside "2nd class" barges, in an area set aside for luggage. The same steamer official I had spoken with earlier came along to eject us since we only had $6-75%-off-discount third class tickets. I managed to finagle an unofficial "upgrade" to second class for only $5 additional each, paid directly to the steamer man. He subsequently scribbled something on each of our tickets, and we had a piece of deck to call our own !! Great ! Of course all of the 2nd class cabins had been booked in advance for several months.

About midnight that night, trying to sleep on the steel deck, with clouds of mosquitoes hovering about, only partially deterred by my rub-on mossie repellent, everything went suddenly to Hades. Hundreds more people came CRASHING down to the river in every taxi, cart and wagon that could move in all of Juba, and all of them were cramming themselves and all of their belongings directly into our tiny luggage area!!! You see, the steamer company had announced that they had outright CANCELED next week's Nile steamer, so all of the folks who thought they had cabin reservations on that trip now found themselves on the deck for this one! Aaargh! Now, finding that I had literally only standing room, with litter and trash already starting to build up around my feet, added to aching guts and other unresolved health challenges, I just could not see myself spending a week squatting here as mosquito fodder. So, for the first and last time in my vagabonding, I copped out. I gave my trip food to the Dutchmen, shouldered my pack, and walked back to the Hotel Africa, giving up on riding the Nile steamer.

Having abandoned my plans to ride the Nile steamer, I walked slowly back to Juba's Hotel Africa, occasionally doubled over with dysentery cramps, carrying all of my worldly belongings. It was about 3am, so I didn't check in, but lay down on the concrete floor for a couple of hours of much needed shuteye. Since it had become apparent that it was time to leave the Sudan, I decided to hop the Sudanese flight to Uganda. Therefore, as soon as the sun came up, I was hustling around trying to get the grasping little bank in Juba to exchange enough money for the ticket. It was a real time stretch, as I didn't want to wait another four days for the next flight, and every transaction operated on "African time". I made it onboard only because the little 13 seat Fokker airliner was running almost empty, and the pilot had heard that I was coming.

## Lake Victoria from the Air

Yep, they held the plane for me. I found my amigo Paul already on board, trying to figure out which of the guys alongside the runway was his Sudanese Government "tail". We took off about 10am for the short flight, which cost me $220, five week's traveling budget. But it was almost worth it. I got to see Lake Victoria from the air, and that freshwater sea is staggeringly large and truly heart-wrenchingly beautiful. Even from our altitude I could not see the southern shore. I can hardly imagine what John Speke, in the 1850s, must have felt when he viewed it. He too was very sick with dysentery when he stood on its bank, the first European ever to do so. That stunning view completed my trip from the Mediterranean up the world's mightiest river, because Lake Victoria's northern exit is the legendary SOURCE OF THE NILE.

We landed at Entebbe, which was new and modern and slick. The empty, echoing terminal was easily the most first-world place I had seen in a long time. (To be exact, ever since I had sneaked into the Nile Hilton two months earlier for the purpose of "appropriating" some otherwise-unobtainable toilet paper.) History buffs will remember that Entebbe is the airfield where, 10 years after I passed through, the Israelis would land commandos and rescue hostages. Paul made connections to Nairobi, but I didn't want to pay for another expensive flight, nor under any circumstances to miss seeing Uganda. I cleared customs easily and found a gear-grinding, gasping bus to the nearby capital city of Kampala.

# IDI AMIN'S UGANDA

The horrible rule of Uganda by Idi Amin was peaking in 1975, and the place was, as a result, falling apart rapidly. Dictator Amin had the bright idea of blaming all of Uganda's troubles on those citizens of Asian ancestry. The Asians did seem to own almost all of the businesses, and that didn't seem fair. His solution was to throw them all out, even though many of those folks of Indian heritage had lived in Uganda for four or five generations. It was a pretty good scam for a few weeks. Clever old Idi gave all of the shops confiscated from the Asians to members of his own tribe. I went into two shops in Kampala, and then gave up on any shopping. In one large general-store-type shop the black proprietor sat behind the cash register waiting for customers. I was the only one inside, and it seemed like the place echoed emptily. All he had for sale were some bars of locally produced high-lye soap and a few Gillette razorblades in their blue paper envelopes. The shelves were bare of anything else. The guy had collected money for all of the stock on the shelves when he took over, and had absolutely no impulse to restock, and apparently no idea how to do so. The other shop I visited was in a similar state, but they still had the remnants of four different items for sale. Broken down vehicles were all over the place. There were five derelicts by the side of the road for every one which was still somehow running. You guessed it. The auto mechanics had also all been citizens of Asian ancestry, and had been ejected from the country with the shop-owners. Another bad result of Idi's misrule was the omnipresence of large numbers of VERY important soldiers strutting around haughtily, obviously above the law. They all had loaded automatic weapons, which combined poorly, in my opinion, with their inflated sense of self-worth. I have NEVER had to show my passport to so many people so often. Every soldier that I passed would scoop up his weapon, saunter across the street to confront me, and demand that I show him my papers. Part of the plan was that I was supposed to give each one a bribe, but I was not playing that game. Therefore the rapacious soldier-parasites were taking up lots of my time trying to wheedle money out of me for the privilege of getting my passport handed back to me.

## Border Crossing Advice

I quickly realized that it was already time to get out of Uganda, and I had only been in the country for a few hours! Bargaining with the driver of a truck with Kenyan tags, I purchased a ride to the border. The driver wanted me to go on with him to Nairobi, but I had realized the importance of only taking rides TO borders, then crossing alone on foot, finding transport again on the other side. If you are linked to a bus or share taxi while crossing a border, everyone is limited to the speed of the SLOWEST passenger, and all can wait for many hours for that person to clear customs. Perhaps more importantly, if the driver is actually smuggling and illicit items are discovered, the guilty party can easily bribe the officials and claim that the contraband belongs to his passenger. By riding a vehicle across a border, one can innocently find oneself in prison. Always crossing borders alone has, over the years, saved me lots of risk and hassle, and I highly recommend it to any future vagabonds.

# ESCAPE TO KENYA

Sitting up front with the driver and his two helpers, we were returning empty to Kenya. We had to stop at "military checkpoints" at least a dozen times for the purpose of bribing the soldiers to allow the truck to pass. I was heartily glad to step over the Kenyan border well after nightfall. On the other side I caught a free ride to Nairobi in another truck. The excellent state of the road allowed me to get some sleep under a tarpaulin in the back of the truck. I awakened at dawn just as we entered the outskirts of Nairobi.

# *Nairobi*

Kenya was much better off than Uganda. The city center was quite modern, and not too filthy, the weather was cool and pleasant, and everything seemed to be working. It reminded me strongly of an American city. I found my way to the then-notorious Iqbal hotel, the rundown central vagabond freak hangout in Nairobi. I checked into an upstairs six-bed room for $1.70, finding three Japanese lone travelers, a white South African vagabond, and my buddy Paul already there! The Japanese guys spent hours just sitting around speaking Japanese to one another, and obviously enjoying it immensely. You could tell it had been a long time since any of the three loners had been able to converse in their cradle language. After eating some of the incredibly heavy and greasy "deep fried semolina baseballs" downstairs at the Iqbal, and having my first HOT shower since Egypt (wonderful), my priority was to get myself healthy. Next morning I located a nearby government-run skin clinic and went inside. It was very clean, and free, and efficiently run, with lots of people there for treatment. I was of course the only foreigner. First, I was compelled to fill out papers, but I left the box marked "tribe" blank. When I handed the form over to one of the nice, English-speaking nurses, she finished filling it in for me. I discovered that I am a member of the American tribe.

## Gangrene Diagnosis

Then I stood in various lines to get treatment. I soon realized that the "skin" clinic was really almost entirely devoted to treating venereal disease. All of the staff automatically assumed that I should be treated for syphilis, and I had some trouble convincing folks that I really had come for a skin ailment, and was not just being shy. I soon learned to immediately point to the open suppurating sores on my feet and toes as my communication opener. As it turned out, it probably was fortunate that I had not spent a week on the Nile Steamer. The doctor said I would likely have lost some toes. Gangrene was the diagnosis (!) and I was given a shot of penicillin, just like everyone else, and some ointment which nobody else received. The wonderful climate of Nairobi and the medicine did the trick, and in a week my feet were healed, and I also recovered from my dysentery.

The day after that I took care of another of my priorities. I heard that the first laundromat in Nairobi had just opened in the "European" suburb. Great, I found my way there on two buses, marched in and washed ALL of my clothes at once, with the exception of my swimsuit! It was great! The expatriate housewives were satisfactorily scandalized by my near-nudity, and they turned up their noses at the horrifyingly dark gray rinse water which issued from the washing machine. I had no idea I had been doing that poor a job of sink-washing my clothes. It was great to have clean duds, and I put them back on right there in front of the dryer while they were still hot.

# Confidence Men

An under-rated feature of being a low budget traveler in Nairobi was that one encountered plenty of confidence men. The con men in Nairobi were at that time the very best in the world, and I speak with some authority on this subject. These guys were expert at pushing EVERY psychological button of their intended victims; pity, greed, friendliness, race guilt, it was all used ruthlessly in positioning the target to cough up some money for a "loan". Perhaps here it would be proper to divulge my personally developed method for identifying confidence men. In a strange town, when a local walks up to you and starts a friendly conversation, how do you tell whether he is genuine or a confidence man? Simple. If, within the first two minutes of acquaintance, a new "friend" asks the following three distinct questions, he is certainly a tourist-preying confidence man. The questions are:

How long have you been in town? Where are you staying? When do you plan to leave?

Now these seem like normal and innocent questions, but what the con man is really asking you is:

Are you already familiar with the local confidence scams? What part of town will I have to avoid after I cheat you? How long will I have to stay away from that part of town?

The above system never failed me. A few true sleaze-balls may not ask the questions at the very beginning, but when someone does, he is unerringly marking himself as a predator.

My Californian friend Paul, whom up to that time I had considered a wise and experienced overlander, fell for a very good scam. A team of three bright, clean young men talked him into "loaning" them $22 so that they could rent handcarts at the market for a day, which they would use to strenuously lug goods around, earning enough money to pay him back and to rent the handcarts again the following day with the putative overall goal of earning enough money so that they could buy their textbooks for school. When he told me the story of his inexplicable gullibility, I just shook my head in amazement. Paul was convinced, offering to bet anyone that his con-men would return the following evening and repay him. I had to prevent the South African from taking him up on the bet. Paul didn't need to feel any more stupid than he already did when they failed to reappear.

Having taken care of the necessities, it was time for me to do some sight-seeing. Not much to see in Nairobi, but I visited the National Museum to have a look. It was interesting, mostly natural history stuff. I found the world's biggest bugs in the collection there. They were truly amazing "walking stick" insects. One of them, I swear, was 9" long !! And their "stick" camouflage was unbelievably good. One of the walking sticks had even grown lovely big thorns on its body to better blend in with its favorite bush. I really wonder how unaided natural selection could have resulted in a camouflage solution that perfect and elegant.

Leaving the museum, my unusually good peripheral vision allowed me to spot someone tall approaching me obliquely from behind. Since there were plenty of other people walking around, this direct blind-side approach already branded him "Conman" for me. A very nice looking young black Kenyan fell into step beside me, wearing a dark-colored lightweight suit, a white shirt, a narrow black tie, and inexpensive, well-polished black shoes. He introduced himself in beautiful English as "Charles" and worriedly asked me if I had seen a school party leaving the museum. Seems that Charles was a teacher from Malindi, a lovely coastal town, and he had come up to the museum with the children from his school on two buses for a field trip, and each bus thought he was on the other bus when they left, and of course his wallet was on the bus, and he was stranded. Charles needed a loan to get back home to Malindi, and invited

147

me to stay free at his house when I visited the coast, when he would pay me back, and told me how wonderful it was to talk to me about his problem, because all of the other white tourists had been quite rude and unfriendly to him. I decided to mess with Charles' head a little bit, and pretended to believe his story completely. I commiserated deeply with him, and admitted to having lots of cash, but wouldn't loan him a single shilling. He walked alongside me for a long time, quite genuinely confused, because all of his instincts said that he had scored big, and that I SHOULD be reaching for my money-belt. But it just wasn't happening that way. We finally parted, Charles still flummoxed, and Chick feeling that he had won a small victory for truth and justice. Some weeks later, when I returned to Nairobi after my self-guided photo safari, you may imagine my delight when I found myself walking down the street behind good old Charles, wearing his identical conman rig. His peripheral vision was apparently not as good as mine. I slipped up beside him and clamped my arm in friendly fashion across his shoulders.

"Charles, it is SO good to see you again! What a shame you still haven't been able to get home to Malindi ! Your students must really miss you by now."

The slimeball detached himself and scuttled away from me as quickly as possible, a smile of chagrin frozen painfully on his face. At that moment I am sure he thanked the heavens that on our previous meeting I had NOT fallen for his con !

## *Busted for dope!*

Turnover at the Iqbal hotel in Nairobi was pretty high, and before long all the Japanese and the South African in our dorm had been replaced by another ubiquitous pair of Dutch guys. One morning I walked to the native market on the outskirts of town for the purpose of buying dope for all of us. Many boys surrounded me when I entered the market area, each wanting to be the interpreter and "guide" for the tourist. It was a decent gig for them, because not only did the guide get a tip from the foreigner, but they got back from the sellers a small cut of everything I spent. I chose the lad who seemed to have the most calm behind his eyes, explained to him that I was uninterested in seeing tourist souvenir junk, and whispered my errand. After hustling into the market quite a distance, we found ourselves in front of a shoddy stall made of reeds. I was a bit surprised to be offered not a small, compact package of shredded dope leaves, but a big, intact bush, dirty roots and all. I crushed some between my fingers and smelled it, then entered into a short successful negotiation. The stall-keeper happily wrapped up my bush in newspapers and twine, (I had obviously overpaid), and I walked back into town with my bulky package, trying to appear inconspicuous.

Arriving at our room at the Iqbal, Paul and the Dutchmen and I fastened the hook on the door. The cleaning guy at the freak hotel was a glowering, muttering, suspicious-looking person, and we didn't particularly want him to spot us while we were doing anything surreptitious. We spent a pleasant half-hour cleaning the dope, separating out the stems and seeds, and balancing open magazines in our laps to catch the "good" parts as our fingers shredded them. Then came a peremptory knock at the door! "Just a minute!" We scurried around stuffing the stems back under the beds, and closing things up to look innocent and casual. I went to the door and unfastened it. As we feared, it was the cleaning man. He came into the room scowling, and I turned around to find one Dutchman repairing his backpack and the other nonchalantly reading a paperback. At that moment, Paul reached over to a stack of magazines, chose one to read, and DUMPED ALL OF THE DUTCHMEN'S' DOPE out of it across the floor! We all froze, open-mouthed in amazement at the perfection of Paul's faux-pas! Finally, the cleaning man broke the spell by crying, "THAT is BHANG!" "Yes", I agreed. "Do you want some Bhang?" "NO!" he hissed, and backed out of the doorway. Bummer. We all checked out within half an hour and I spent that night sleeping on the floor of the youth hostel.

## *Photo Safari into the Veldt*

Before I had been in Nairobi very long I found a used car rental outfit called "Oddjob's" and arranged to rent a six-year old VW bug and a pair of worn-out small tents for two weeks. I had my California driver's license certified by the Kenyan Ministry of Transport. Then handmade signs were posted at the Iqbal hotel, the YMCA, and the Youth Hostel soliciting additional bodies to share the car for a photo safari around Kenya and Tanzania. Paul joined up, as well as a Canadian gent named Bill whom I had originally bumped into during a khamseen dust storm in Egypt. The final member of our little safari turned out to be a Brit medical student named Ian, on holiday in Kenya. Great!

Two mornings after the "Bhang" fiasco, the VW was collected and our Safari rendezvoused, as per the plan, in front of the Iqbal. We four stalwarts loaded our gear (there was no luggage rack, so storage was extremely limited) and I drove south for most of the morning to Amboseli game park. Our first day on photo safari was completely amazing! Driving around Amboseli, only 150 miles south of Nairobi, we saw baboons, gazelles, antelopes, guinea hens, hippos, elephants, rhino, zebra, wildebeest, lions, warthogs, and wild water buffalo. WOW! I found that one can really NOT imagine how wonderful the game parks are without actually going there to visit them. Nope, sorry, but Lion Country Safari African Theme Park is not even a patch on the real thing!

The second day we crossed over into Tanzania, and that night we camped in Arusha park, in the foothills around majestic Kilimanjaro. I was awakened in the middle of the night by a crunching and thrashing nearby. I came out of the tent to watch an elephant enthusiastically eating a bush within 60 feet of our tent. It was noisy, and sleeping was out of the question until he sauntered away. I did wonder how the elephants knew not to step on those insignificant little canvas tent-prisms in the dark.

The following morning I was lying half awake, and became aware of a commotion, with the earth shaking just a little. It became louder and stronger, and then the front wall of the tent that Bill and I shared leaned inward. The noise was moving farther away as I stuck my head out of the tent. I saw the south end of a big Water Buffalo going north at good speed. He had passed so close that he had kicked out the tent peg which was guying the front of the tent!!

Three evenings later, the "campground" at the edge of Ngorongoro Crater game park was our stopping point. It really was only a field with a few trash cans chained to a post. We were the only visitors when we arrived in early afternoon, and, after looking into and across the amazing crater, about nine miles across and 1500 feet deep, we pitched our little waist-high tents.

# Ohio State East African Zoological Study

To my surprise, a full-sized modern bus appeared, and parked not far away. It promptly disgorged 30 Ohio State students, whose parents had paid many thousands of dollars so that their little darlings could be chauffeured around East Africa for most of the summer, and receive college credit for it! Now that is REALLY a good gig! While unloading was going on, all eight of the male Ohio State students wandered over to our camp to stand around the campfire and gripe and whine about how they had been camping with those 22 young women for three weeks already, and NONE of the guys had managed to get close to ANY of the gals! This information captured our full and complete attention. Each of the four of us had the same series of thoughts:

-These guys do seem quite lame and ineffectual, therefore I admire the taste of the ladies.
-Since it has been 3 weeks since these gals have been close to a man, and since they all believe that they are on an "adventure", it follows that they might be ready for a helping of each.
-Ergo, we may have just crossed into the Happy Hunting Ground.

Soon the Ohio State girls drifted over to visit in twos and threes, and Glory Be, our wild fantasy became fact. Serious interest was shown in the only four real men available, and the odds were such that several young ladies were openly competing for the attention of each of us. After a few of my stories about solo overland vagabonding, Open Season was declared on nubile mid-western American females. Yowee! The critical limitation to our lascivious horizons was the regrettable lack of privacy. We had two 2-man tents for four of us, and the ladies had four 6-person tents for 22 of them. Oh well. I dare not imagine how crushed the egos of the Ohio State guys must have been by all of this. After careful consideration, I chose an unusually-friendly dishwater-blond named Jennifer. We chatted into the night around our little campfire. And there we heard, from their professor/guide, the story of this exact campsite on the previous year's trip.

When the bus had arrived in 1974, there had been yet another of the omnipresent duos of overlanding Netherlanders squatting there. These guys intended to sleep out under the stars. I had heard that this was not recommended in Masai tribal areas, such as Ngorongoro. The picturesque Masai, you see, have the rather strange funerary custom of leaving their fresh dead next to known hyena trails. This has the unintended side effect of training the hyenas to eat anyone they find lying out on the ground at night.

As additional background, Ngorongoro Crater is the place where the definitive studies of hyena behavior were made. These studies proved that hyenas, far from being merely scavengers of other animal kills, actually hunt very effectively in packs, bringing down large game. It was found that more often than not, the local lions, being bigger and more dangerous, actually chase the hyenas away from the hyena kills, thereby reversing the previously accepted roles of hunter/scavenger.

## Hyena Encounters

The professor had explained all this to last year's Dutchmen, and had offered them a place to sleep in the bus. But they, having come all the way from South Africa, figured that they knew everything, and slept out anyway. One of them awoke just in time to get his hands up in front of his face, so that the powerful jaws of the hyena standing over him bit through both of his hands instead of grabbing him by the face to drag him away! His screams woke the camp, and they spent the next day trying to get the injured Dutchman to a place where his mangled hands could be treated!!

That night I was awakened by a snuffling at the outside of the sloping pup tent wall, inches from my face. I slapped the tent, and the snuffler went away, but only temporarily, and soon was again nosing the canvas. I could smell its breath, and figured it was a hyena. We had previously seen the nasty little striped hyenas, just over knee high, with their hindquarters only a foot off the ground. I wanted to get back to sleep, figured there were a couple of striped hyenas outside, and decided that I would go out and make some noise and chase them away. So I quietly got out of my sleeping bag, gripped my new Masai war club, and crouched inside while silently unzipping the tent door. Bursting out into the glaring moonlight in my underwear, hollering fiercely and waving my arms over my head, I quickly realized that I had made three serious miscalculations.

1. There were not a few hyenas outside, there were more than 15.
2. There were no striped hyenas, but instead spotted hyenas, the first I had seen. Each of these critters was the size of a BIG German Shepherd.
3. They did NOT run away, but looked at me with great interest, moonlight glinting in their eyes!

So I stopped and shut up. Bill, awakened by my noise, was loudly calling out "What's going on ????? Are you all right ?????", but, being a clever gent, he was NOT coming out of the tent to investigate. At that point I figured it would be awfully ignominious to just slink cravenly back inside the tent, so I shook my war club, yelled again, and moved towards the largest group of the big predators. To my IMMENSE relief, they all loped calmly away, looking curiously back over their shoulders at me.

The next day, my new friend Jennifer was declared "camp guard" while all of the other students went down into the crater to see the animals. Since this campsite had such a dangerous reputation, I declared myself our camp guard while the rest of "Safari Iqbal" drove down into the crater. When we broke camp the following morning, I got an itinerary of the Ohio State East African Zoological Tour from Jennifer, and filed it away for future reference.

## Olduvai Gorge

Not far from Ngorongoro is Olduvai gorge, which I coerced my companions into visiting. The Leakeys had already moved on to greener fossil beds to the north around Lake Rudolph. As my buddies expected, there wasn't much to see; a circle of stones identified as a very ancient fire circle, and a little one-room shack museum with some bored guards. We were the only visitors that day. I was allowed to hold some of the stone tools used by our far far distant ancestors. Really, I think it was more of a pilgrimage for me than a tourist attraction.

Ian
Scouting

We visited many game parks. Our navigating drill went as follows. We find a climbable tree, and I, as the strongest, boost Ian, who had binoculars, up into the lower branches. He climbs to a good spot, and then scouts for animals, relaying the information down to us. Shortly we drive in the indicated direction, all eyes peeled. It worked very well. Whenever we wanted to find the big carnivores, we could just drive to the bottom of the nearest chimney of circling vultures. The lions were very impressive, sitting or walking regally with their bloody muzzles, ignoring the sputtering VW can of humans.

Ian, Bill, Paul, Chick

Lions Ignore Safari Iqbal

Bulgarian Film meets
Kenyan Development

Once as we came up a gentle rise, following a faint vehicle track, I hit the brakes, and all of us gasped with astonishment! There in front of us was a MASSIVE herd of wildebeest, all moving left to right! There must have been 5000 of the critters, and we drove carefully through the moving herd. The view would have been unchanged a hundred thousand years ago. It was a vision right out of the Pleistocene!

On another occasion I used the VW to chase an ostrich. The auto is faster than the big bird, but not nearly as maneuverable! Whenever I felt that we were catching up, the ostrich would just go perpendicularly right or left in a heartbeat, and it took me a few hundred yards to get turned around again. The ostrich was not afraid of us in the least. When I tried unsuccessfully to get a couple of rhinos to chase us, the rest of the safari summarily voted that Ian, with the only other official driving license, would henceforward be the sole approved driver whenever BIG animals were sighted. Spoilsports! That would have made a really great story.

Soon we fell into a daily rhythm, breaking camp and packing up in the morning, driving around seeing amazing things all through the day, and finding somewhere to camp in the evening. After pitching our two little pup tents, Ian and Paul usually took the car to the nearest Game Lodge for a big fancy expensive dinner, since they seemed to have much larger traveling budgets than I did. Meanwhile Bill and I would remain at the camp and cook up semolina or beans for dinner, over a little campfire.

# Stampede

One evening, camped out in the open veldt beside a track, we had finished our dinner and Bill and I were standing beside the remains of our fire, chatting quietly until our companions would reappear, usually rather drunk. It was completely overcast, and a very dark night. We couldn't make out the horizon, and the only things that existed in our black world were the tiny red dots of embers in the fire and the end of Bill's cigarette. I have seldom before or since been outside in a night so opaquely dark. Suddenly we were completely surrounded by thundering hooves! Large numbers of BIG fast-moving animals were roaring past us on both sides, many passing between us and the nearby tents! We couldn't see a thing, and I was spinning around trying to get the little flashlight out of the breast pocket of my denim jacket! When I finally switched it on, all that could be seen were the clouds of dust which clogged our noses, and thousands of hoof-prints! The herd had already passed! This was a really exciting occurrence. We never did get to see which type of animals had stampeded all around within a few feet of us. However, quite fortunately, we also never saw whatever it was that those galloping animals were running away FROM! After that when just the two of us were out in the middle of the savanna, unarmed, with no vehicle, I did feel a little bit more exposed.

## Hepatitis Diagnosis

Poor Paul seemed to be feeling sicker and sicker. I looked into his eyes on the 10th day of Safari, and realized that the whites were going yellow. Bad sign. After seeing Thompson's Falls, we broke off the journey a few days early and returned to Nairobi. Sure enough, Paul had hepatitis. As far as I know, none of the rest of us came down with it. Checked into the Iqbal again, I shopped the local junkyards and managed to find a VW tailpipe to replace the one we had lost during one of my more enthusiastic driving episodes. I jammed it into place and returned the car to Oddjobs. When the four of us settled up our accounts, the entire 11 day trip, including car rental, equipment rental, food, camping fees, petrol, entrance fees, everything, had cost me a total of $121 USD. Cheap Bill was out of pocket slightly less, and Ian and Paul had spent considerably more. I dare to claim that Safari Iqbal was the very best 11-dollar-per-day safari which ever was organized.

I had been hearing good stories from other travelers about the tropical coast of Kenya. It proved easy to hitchhike from Nairobi down to the coast at Mombasa, along a modern, well-maintained highway. Mombasa is much older than Nairobi, and more interesting. One tourist attraction was Fort Jesus, a lumpy, unprepossessing three-hundred-year-old waterfront fortification made of coral blocks. It was originally built by Portuguese traders in the years before the Sultan of Zanzibar kicked the Portuguese out of East Africa. The business community was an interesting blend of East Indian and Arab stock. Being a port town, sailors of every imaginable description abounded.

Ladies of the evening in Mombasa proved to be very aggressive and persistent, unwilling to accept my "No thanks" response to their overtures. One flashing eyed young woman snatched away the sweater I was carrying, and retreated, teasing and beckoning, into a nearby doorway. It was a chore to retrieve my garment while maintaining my dignity. And this was at 9 o'clock in the morning! Walking around central Mombasa I spied familiar faces. Three of the Ohio State ladies strolled out of the post office. I wasn't too surprised to see them, since I had memorized the schedule of their bus tour, so my presence in Mombasa on that particular day was a bit less than coincidental. The gals seemed happy to find me, and led me a few blocks to where their bus was parked. They hid me in the rear of the bus until Jennifer boarded. She was shocked but seemed pleased to have me reappear, delivering a big unexpected hug right there between the seats in front of God and everybody! When Jennifer asked me which way I was headed, I said that I had heard about a particularly nice beach south of Mombasa called Twiga. Another amazing coincidence! That was exactly where the Ohio State folks were headed that afternoon, planning to camp for the next four days! So by popular acclaim, the professor in charge made exceptions to quite a few tour rules, and I got a free ride to Twiga (means "giraffe" in Swahili, I'm told) on the East Africa Zoological Study bus.

## Twiga Beach

Twiga is really a lovely place, quite near the equator. A simple, laid-back low lodge was surrounded by lots of big trees, a dozen nice bungalows and a campground. Since June was off season, it was almost deserted. I rented a two-bedroom bungalow for $3 total per night, and two of the students immediately moved into the second room, tired of living in the tents. The bungalow was large and airy, the main external walls being made out of a checkerboard pattern of coral blocks and air. While this construction style did manage to deny access to uninvited humans, it provided hot and cold running monkeys for free! Quite a troop of those little critters lived in the trees at Twiga, and they entered and exited at will. A big lockable zinc-lined box was provided in the kitchen to keep the food secure from monkey raiders. Time spent at Twiga was idyllic. In the mornings, a procession of beautiful Kenyan girls visited each bungalow with baskets on their heads selling ripe mangoes, or fresh pastries, or coconuts, or chocolate bars, or pineapples, or other tropical fruit. A low reef 150 yards offshore enclosed a small lagoon in which it was pleasant to wade and collect shells.

The days were beautiful, with a nice breeze always coming either on or offshore. Every afternoon about 3:00, like clockwork, a good big thunderstorm came in off the Indian Ocean and it rained like crazy for an hour, and then reliably stopped. During the storms, everyone sat in the big thatched patio of Twiga Lodge, reading and talking. Many hours after dark were pleasantly spent sitting talking on the beach. It was a nice, comfortable social scene. Twiga was the first place on my travels where I truly felt as if I were on holiday. One afternoon I returned to our bungalow to find at least 30 monkeys sitting on the thatched roof. Bad sign. I came closer to see that the alpha male monkey had stolen a half loaf of bread, complete with its waxed paper wrapper, from our kitchen, and was sitting on the ridge pole eating it. The other monkeys were clustered around in hopes that he would drop some, or would get full before the bread ran out. Realizing my assigned role in this scene, I shook my fist at the thief, calling out in jest "You scruffy monkey, give us back our bread!" The regal old gray male then displayed his sense of humor by finishing the last of the bread, crumpling up the wrapper into a ball, and disdainfully throwing it down directly at my feet.

## Sea Snakes

While wading at Twiga the next morning, I spotted a colony of the famous local sea snakes just inside the reef. Sea snakes, according to reliable reports, are SO poisonous that anyone bitten dies within three steps! And there they were, in the calm waist-deep water, four or five pairs of bright black eyes on long, slender bodies sticking up out of holes in the bottom, swaying to and fro as the water moved about them. They didn't appear too aggressive, and I made a mental note of the colony location for future reference. "Arachnid Andy" was the name secretly assigned to one of the socially introverted Ohio State guys by his fellows. Andy was a guy who would get really excited and happy whenever I told him about an interesting snake or spider I had seen somewhere in the past. He would whip out his notebook, furiously take notes on the sighting, and demand more and more details. He did know a tremendous amount about snakes and spiders, and was the acknowledged local expert.

I detected an opportunity to improve my masculine image with the bevy of Ohio State females by capturing one of the deadly sea snakes as a gift for Arachnid Andy. I walked a short distance inland and found a nice hard stick, about 18" long and a quarter inch in diameter. I whittled a shallow groove around one end, tied a piece of my mono-filament line into the groove, and fed the loose end back under the band, making an effective little noose which would tighten when I pulled on the loose end of the mono-filament. With my jury-rigged catching stick and a mason jar, I waded carefully out to the sea snake colony. The snakes all pulled themselves back into their burrows when they sensed my approach. I squatted down nearby, with my chin in the water, and positioned my little noose over the entrance to one burrow. Before long a smooth head peeked out cautiously. I jerked the line and caught him right behind the head. He wrapped his body around the catching stick as I pulled him out of the burrow.

With the poisonous end of the stick in the jar full of sea water, I loosened the line, and my captive freed himself and swam rapidly around. I removed the stick and secured the screw lid on the jar. IT WORKED! Just like the plan! AMAZING! Shortly I was the center of a knot of cooing young women, listening to my manly story, and admiring the dangerous-looking sea snake as we waited for Andy to return. Ah, good, there he came, striding gawkily along, headed past us towards his tent.

"Andy, I've caught a sea snake for you!"

Arachnid Andy's head snapped around to view my proffered jar. Never even slowing down, he marched quickly past.

"Thass a EEL" he said dismissively. No question that he was right. My newly-earned "brave hunter" status deflated. I released my inoffensive little eel near his home shortly thereafter.

## Lamu Island

After finally waving good-bye to my friends from Ohio as they headed back to Nairobi and then home, I bought a bus ticket up the long, muddy coastal road towards Lamu, a tiny island off Kenya's northern coast. Everyone on the bus seemed to be either selling or chewing "speed weed", the bitter leaves also called "qat", or "kyat" by some. I chewed quite a bit of it myself, as it was interesting and inexpensive. The effect was a slight, disconnected feeling of euphoria after considerable intake of speed weed. I can understand why the Somalis tend to fire all of their weapons into the air every afternoon.

The old bus, even with its huge double rear wheels, got stuck in the mud several times. All the male passengers, it seemed, were expected to assist in pushing it out, and I helped along with the rest. Due to my inexperience in these matters, I first chose a pushing position just behind the wheels, resulting in much hilarity from my companions when I found myself covered up to the waist with brown sticky mud ejected by the spinning tires. Eventually we reached a nasty, smelly little pier on the mainland shore, and rode an overloaded, decrepit sailboat to the island, easily visible 20 kilometers offshore.

Boat to Lamu Island

Lamu town was very picturesque and interesting. Plenty of buildings dated from the period 100 to 300 years ago, when Lamu was a major slaving port, providing human property to the Middle East. The architecture is not exactly Arabian, and not exactly anything else, but a fascinating blend of local traditions and original design. Intricately carved wooden doors and door-frames were to be seen on every street. A Zanzibari fortress occupied the center, and old muzzle-loading cannons were scattered everywhere around the town. Food was excellent and very cheap. Fresh lobster tails could be purchased for 60 cents per pound, and cooked up at any of the local cafes for only a few cents per meal. Amu Lodging, facing the waterfront close to the center of town, was a bargain at 61 cents for my own room, with a big 4-poster bed with FULL MOSQUITO NETTING! I immediately fell in love with mosquito nets which wrap protectively around a bed, because they obviate the need to fumigate oneself all night with the toxic fumes from burning mosquito coils. Yes, on the magical isle of Lamu, one could live luxuriously for $2 per day.

## *Unexpected Romance*

Lamu got electricity from a big generator which could be heard all over the town. In theory it operated from dusk to midnight every night, but in practice blackouts were common.

One evening I was sitting on one of two big swings on the Amu's second-story porch overlooking the harbor. An hour earlier I had met an Australian woman named Elwyn, who was chatting sitting next to me. There were a few Kenyans on the porch, and three people on the second swing just across from ours, and the night was pleasant. Suddenly the generator stopped, throwing the town into inky black silence. Elwyn astonished me by slipping her slender body under my right arm, planting herself in my lap and delivering a big, wet, penetrating kiss! That moment is still the most direct come-on I've ever personally experienced. The following morning I was somewhat nonplussed to discover that Elwyn had a boyfriend who was also living at the Amu. He had gone somewhere for three days, and my new friend had taken good advantage of his absence. That seemed a shame, because I was by then rather fond of the woman, and now, to keep my life simple, it was obvious that I should disappear from Lamu before the return of the cuckolded boyfriend. But at least I enjoyed another 48 hours in that paradise, body-surfing on the far side of the island with Elwyn in the daytime and hiding from the mosquitoes at night. Actually, I felt a bit dishonorable for not breaking things off immediately.

## Malaria Diagnosis

As I was preparing to leave Lamu island I began to feel lousy. I was getting headaches, my joints also ached, and bright sunlight became progressively less bearable. I bussed back to Mombasa and after a night there, hitch-hiked up into the cooler high savanna, checking once more into the Iqbal hotel in Nairobi. By that time it was obvious that I was pretty sick, as I was sweating copiously, and unable to keep much in my stomach other than water. I dragged myself out to a local doctor. Sure enough, I was down with Malaria. I guess the mosquito nets didn't do a good enough job.

It seemed that everything that could go wrong WENT! Every joint ached, my old joint surgeries fell apart, my neck was too stiff to move, I was nauseous, dizzy, farty, burpy, diahrrea-y, very very feverish, with cold shivering chills ! But none of that was the worst. I have a very high pain threshold, and was taking two kinds of potent pain-killing medications, but the headaches which lived IN my eyes, were very nearly unbearable. It felt as if my eyeballs would be the size of tennis balls if they weren't constrained by my skull. The inexpensive Kenyan doctor prescribed quinine and rest. I moved into a more expensive room at the Iqbal which had only two beds in it and settled down to ride out the disease. The killer headaches and hallucinations which I suffered for the next few days are still the most powerful and most amazing I have ever experienced. I lay in the cheap bed, teeth occasionally clacking, shaking and sweating with fever, afraid to close my eyes because of the terrifying disjointed full-action-color visions which always took over. With most hallucinations I have found that I could sit back and watch, aware that they were unreal, and that they would pass. For some reason I couldn't achieve any "distance" from these, they were too immediate and always real and threatening. With a half hour of mental preparation, I could just barely get myself up a few times a day to drink water and to use the toilet. Fortunately, after three hellish days the fever broke, and after four I could stagger out to buy crackers and ginger ale. Malaria is no fun, I can assure you, but neither is it the end of a vagabond's world.

As I recovered from my first bout with Malaria, Ethiopia beckoned. Once healed, I therefore shouldered my backpack and hitch-hiked north from Nairobi towards Moyale, a little border post between Kenya and Ethiopia. Hitch hiking was slow, but workable. That evening, after 3 rides, I bought a cheap, uncomfortable, bug-infested bed in a village at the center of Marsabit game reserve. I found myself marooned there for the whole following day.

## Cross-Cultural Pollution

In the morning, standing beside the road going north out of town, thumbing the very few vehicles that passed, the local children gathered around me. I chatted with the nice kids, and soon grew bored, so I picked up one of the funny little 6" diameter dry "weed" gourds growing alongside the road. My audience was very interested in this, because the locals didn't eat them, or use them for anything. I cut a big plug out of the top around the stem, scraped out all of the dried seeds inside, and proceeded to cut a jack-o-lantern face with my pocketknife. I gave the carved gourd to the kid who spoke the best English, and WOW, what a response! This was obviously a COMPLETELY NEW idea! All of the children got really excited, and each had to have his or her own little jack-o-lantern!

Jack-O-Lanterns
Cross Cultural Pollution

After I carved about 5 gourds, each with its own individualized face, and kids had run off home with their prizes, the elders came around to see what weird things I was doing while standing there looking for a ride. Some of them took out their knives, and soon it seemed that half the village population was busy cutting strange faces into the sides of the trash gourds, and displaying them proudly. I state without fear of contradiction, that the faces I personally carved were the best, but then, I had a 24-year-head-start on the Kenyans in Halloween-pumpkin-carving. The following morning I found adults and kids already carving gourds near my spot beside the road. I finally got a lift with a jeep full of government youth service employees, and threw myself into the back. Dozens of people waved good-bye to me briefly, and then turned immediately back to their carving. As Marsabit disappeared in the road dust, I wondered whether perhaps my popular little jack-o-lanterns would become part of an obscure local tradition. Someday I will have to go back and find out.

# FOUR EASY WAYS TO FIND ONESELF KILLED IN MYSTERIOUS ETHIOPIA

For months I had been collecting info on Ethiopia, via exchange of stories with other vagabonds. Ethiopia had a reputation for being a relatively dangerous place for overland tourists. It seemed that in each section of Ethiopia there was a different reason to encounter a violent death. A popular uprising was in full bloom in the extreme North of the country. In 1952, Hallie Selassie, the emperor of Ethiopia, had been allowed to annex Italy's ex-Red-sea-colony of Eritrea, but the Eritreans had never been enthusiastic with this idea, and in 1975 were in open rebellion against the "occupying" Ethiopian troops. Therefore the whole northern part of the country was closed to travel, and the main road to Asmara, the capital, was usually closed due to rebel military activity. (Eritrea finally won its independence in 1993.)

In the Eastern regions of Ethiopia, the Muslim Somali tribes were restive, and there was sporadic small scale fighting with generally Christian government forces. As predicted, in the 70s, these simmering tensions finally broke into full scale anti-government warfare, supported by military forces from Somalia.  The tribes were brutally suppressed, using Soviet supplied tanks, and the Ogaden area is still part of Ethiopia.

In the central mountainous regions, bands of "Shifta" occasionally ambushed travelers. The Shifta were armed groups of either local patriots or bandits, depending upon whom you asked. I heard a second-hand story of a Dutch vagabond who had awakened in his roadside camp with a big lump on his head, badly beaten, wearing only his skivvies and socks, with all of his belongings missing and his traveling companion dead beside him. Shifta had attacked with clubs as they slept, and neither ever knew what hit him. Normally I would have taken such second-hand stories with a big dose of salt, but this one was gravely reported to me by the officials at the Ethiopian government tourist office in the capital city of Addis Ababa!

The most colorful story involved the southwest regions, around Lake Rudolph and the Omo river valley. The large tribal groups living in that area, according to the stories, had an interesting tradition for becoming engaged. When a young man decides to get married, tradition dictates that he must present to his intended the severed penis of a man whom he has personally killed ! She, in turn, suspends the gift by a string so that as she grinds grain, it bumps against her forehead with each stroke, thus assuring, in some mysterious fashion, her future fertility. Now this story I found SO outlandish that I mentally discarded it as a fabrication.

A few days later, once I was settled into Addis, I found a dozen nice Ethiopian technical students staying temporarily at the same cheap hotel. In chatting with them, I found out that all of them were of the Omo tribe, and came from the Lake Rudolph region, and that their school had let out and closed the dorms for the holidays six days previously. When I asked why they were hanging around Addis instead of going home they informed me that in a few more days another bigger technical school would let out, and they were waiting for those guys so they could all go home together in a big self-protective group of about 40. They confirmed every detail of the "penis as betrothal present" story, and assured me that a white penis would be perfectly acceptable. They traveled to and from school in perpetual fear of becoming such a gift for one of their matrimonially-minded neighbors! Yowee!

When I finally reached Moyale three days out of Nairobi, I ran into a substantial hassle. I had originally gotten my Ethiopian visa in Khartoum, intending to enter Ethiopia through Metema, and later had gotten the Ethiopian embassy in Nairobi to amend my visa, crossing out the "Metema only" notation and initialing and stamping the change. At the Moyale border post, however, the guy in charge told me that was no good, and I had either to go back to the Sudan and enter through Metema, or go back to Nairobi and get a completely new visa. Bad scene. Several hours later I was still sitting politely in his office, not quite willing to admit defeat, and not willing to try a bribe. For the twentieth time he waved my passport at me disdainfully, and finally looked closely at the initials on the visa amendment. "AH! Did you speak with Mr. Habibi? Yes, this is his writing! Mr. Habibi is an old and close friend of mine!" And in short order my passport got the necessary stamps to allow me to enter Ethiopia. Unexpected good luck.

On the far side of the border, where folks drive on the right side of the road again, just like in the US, I bought a ride to Addis Ababa on an Ethiopian bus. This proved to be a mistake, because the buses in that country invariably play horrible screeching-nasally-whining local music through speakers scattered throughout the bus, at extremely high decibel levels. After only 20 minutes of this I had a headache, and the bus ride was nearly three days! In addition, many Ethiopians chain smoke horrible cheap cigarettes, which made the atmosphere inside the buses perfectly foul. After this learning experience I always tried to buy rides on top of trucks instead of in buses. The prices were similar, and though it was sometimes awfully cold up in the open-topped luggage box on top of the cab of a truck, it was a much better ride.

I made some English speaking friends on this bus, by shouting little messages to one another above the caterwauling cacophony. Mr. Georgi, a Christian Ethiopian, and Bennet, a young Watusi Kenyan, were also going to Addis.

## Ethiopian Hotels

We stopped well after dark at a dusty town called Yabelo where I rented a bed in a tiny single room under the stairs. I was asked by the clerk to choose a woman from a sample of three ladies lounging in the "lobby" area, two of whom were young and reasonably attractive. Smiling knowingly, Mr. Georgi translated for me, and I quickly memorized how to say, in Amharic, "I'm really tired". Then we re-negotiated, the bed price dropped by ninety cents, and I spent the night peacefully. Apparently, however, the girls all had passkeys, and I was awakened the next morning by the prettiest long-legged ebony woman climbing naked into bed with me! She reckoned since I had rested, I wouldn't be tired anymore! Then I really had to talk fast, and I know she thought I was some sort of sexual misfit because I rejected her. Ethiopia also has a reputation for various exotic varieties of endemic incurable sexually transmitted diseases. In addition, my firm belief is that sex and money should never both be included in the same interaction. I subsequently learned that ladies of the evening have reasonably high status in Ethiopia. Prostitution is considered a perfectly honorable profession. This is said to derive from the Queens of Sheba, who used their sexual favors as a tool in ancient diplomacy. In Ethiopia I actually found it difficult to get only a bed with no hooker included, and the pattern of being awakened by a naked girl repeated itself once farther north.

# Home Brewed Liquer

At a rest stop the next day, only a few hours south of Addis, in a dirt-floored, rough-plank-tabled shop, I bought a round of tea for my friends on the bus. After a busy discussion with the woman who ran the place, Mr. Georgi announced that he would treat me to some of the local home-brewed-liqueur, which had a long, musical name in Amharic. She brought out a small shot glass half full of clear distilled fluid, which smelled just a whiff like methanol. We shared it around the table, and when I wet my lips with it, the drink did seem to be very powerful. Mr Georgi poured a little drop of it out onto the wooden table. The bead glistened there, held together by surface tension, as he lighted it with his cigarette lighter. As I watched amazed, the drop burned with an almost invisible blue flame only 1/16th of an inch high, until it was COMPLETELY consumed, leaving no residue! I asked what the name meant in English, and Mr. Georgi, after some thought, translated from Amharic. "It means", he said, "Kill Me Quickly".

Ethiopia seemed to take perverse satisfaction in keeping out of step with the rest of the world. They still adhered to long-defunct Byzantine calculations on the birth of Christ, so while the rest of the world believed it was 1975, in Ethiopia it was only 1967. The Ethiopian year has 13 months, with our September 11th as their New Year's Day. And Ethiopian time is six hours ahead of world standard, so 10 am everywhere else is 4 o'clock in Ethiopia.

## Addis Ababa

I found Addis Ababa, the capital city of the country, to be strange in several ways. Since there was so much tension in the country, soldiers abounded, and everyone was searched by the military before being allowed into any major building. The architecture was really hit and miss. By far most of Addis was just tumble-down slums, but right in the center of town, big glass and steel 10 story hotels sat beside garbage covered empty lots where herds of goats grazed. Enormous numbers of beggars were everywhere, quite heart-rending to look at, and extremely persistent, a supplicating pack of them following me wherever I went in the city.

## Central Tourist Office

I searched out the country's only tourist office in Addis. It was well stocked with glossy pamphlets, and there really were lots of quite amazing things to see in the country. But the tourist officials concentrated on talking me OUT of traveling overland in Ethiopia, and they were quite determined. They told me about the Shiftas, and the danger in the northern areas of the country, and showed me a list of the names, nationalities, and death dates of exactly 12 overland travelers whom they knew had been killed there in the past year! And those were only the ones they knew about! A dozen a year isn't many to lose, until one realizes that at any given moment there were probably only 20 western vagabonds in the whole country, and then it becomes a substantial proportion. By my calcs, between one in 10 and one in 20 of all vagabonds through Ethiopia in 1974 / 1975 found their grave there.

## The Shoa

The Shoa hotel, in the middle of the red light district in Addis, was the city's traditional "freak" lodging. It was a ramshackle two-story wooden building around a courtyard with a few tired shrubs, and my bed was comfortable and not too filthy. There were half a dozen Farangi (white foreigners) living there when I arrived, and some of them had been settled in for quite some time. I find myself uncomfortable relating it, but the Shoa was a pedophiles paradise. Starched-collared uniformed schoolgirls stopped by the Shoa every afternoon on their way home from school to make a little pocket money selling themselves to the hotel guests for less than a dollar. The older professional ladies based in the Shoa were very jealous of the competition, and tried unsuccessfully to keep the schoolgirls out. On July 3rd it occurred to me that there might be some sort of an Independence Day celebration at the local American consulate, so I went there to ask. Yep, there was a bash planned, but only for big-shots. Random US citizens were definitely not invited. Or maybe it was just longhaired, travel-worn US citizens who were unwelcome.

## Blue Nile Gorge

So instead, on the morning of the Fourth of July, I boarded a truck to Bahir Dar, three days north through the mountains. The first day's travel was nice, sightseeing from the luggage box on top of the cab, through fertile fields and hills. In the afternoon we pulled up to the edge of Blue Nile Gorge, and looked down. My heart leapt up into my throat! WOW! What an amazing natural wonder! It is a mile deep (as deep as the Grand Canyon), only one mile wide, and blindingly green! We went down switchbacks for several hours, arriving at the well-guarded little bridge at the bottom 45 minutes too late to be allowed across. Because of rebel-cum-bandit depredations, all travel between 6pm and 6am was forbidden throughout most of the country. Well, that sucked, because there was nothing there at the bottom of the gorge except a guard building on one side. The truck crew were sleeping in the cab, so I tried to sleep on the truck load, but when a really long, hard rain started falling, I moved to the asphalt underneath the truck. The pavement was still hot, it was extremely humid, and CLOUDS of mosquitoes had also hidden under the truck from the rain. They casually ignored the gobs of repellent I used, so I spent a supremely uncomfortable night.

All of the following day it rained intermittently, and people got on and off the truck, using it as a local bus. I talked the driver into letting me lie on the boards behind the seats in the cab, and partially caught up on my sleep that way. At one point I opened my eyes to see the profiles of two beautiful Ethiopian women sitting in the passenger seat of the cab. One of them turned and spotted me. When I winked at her, she SCREAMED and jumped towards the door, pointing and spouting a torrent of loud terrified Amharic! The driver said something to her in that language which calmed her down, and soon she came back to play with my long straight hair. I could tell from his tone that the driver had said, "Yeah, yeah, I KNOW there's a Farangi behind the seat, now relax."

## Fly Capital of the World

Bahir Dar turned out to be a nasty little town in a really beautiful place. It sits on the southeastern shore of Lake Tana, Ethiopia's largest lake. There are more than 30 little islands in the lake, and many of those have old churches or monasteries on them. Simple boats made out of bundles of a papyrus-like reed plied the clear, still water. Bahir Dar was also, at the time, the fly capital of the world. When I climbed down from the truck a cloud of flies immediately enveloped me. The local people didn't even notice them anymore, and I found it very disturbing to watch flies walking all over and around small children's eyes without causing any response. I sat at a small table in front of a cafe at the open area which served Barhar Dar for a transport hub. Having ordered a soda, it was nearly impossible to drink any without also ingesting a fly or two as they swarmed around the open bottle and my mouth. The table itself had a fly at least every 1" in any dimension. Just sweeping my hand over the table I could catch a dozen at once as they flew upwards. I found the omnipresence of Bahir Dar's flies rather horrible.

## Blue Nile Falls

I tried to find transport going to Blue Nile Falls, said to be one of the most amazing natural sites in all of Africa. But due to Shifta depredations, petrol was very short in Bahir Dar, and the bus that went that direction wasn't running. For a few hours I made good use of my Frisbee, and again it was a novelty. I had several dozen youngsters playing with it in the open area, and nobody had ever seen one before. They learned to throw it, under my tutelage, very quickly, and crowds of people and flies competed for it whenever it landed. The following day I did find a van operating as a share taxi which was headed that direction, but since I was a tourist, I was required to pay $25 for a 20 mile ride, when I knew that everybody else was paying 65 cents. Well, I wouldn't stand for that, so I just stayed there hunkered down on the floor of the van, waiting for the owners to agree, and accept my 65 cent payment. They out-waited me, and finally I took pity on the other folks who were waiting to depart, and debarked. The operators of the van proved that they would rather drive off without me than to miss the chance of really cheating me properly. I'm sure they thought that I would crack and pay outrageous sums on the following day. They were wrong, and I was very disappointed. As a result, I did not see Blue Nile Falls, though I had come so far and gotten SO close. Perhaps it was all for the best, as I heard later that a band of Shifta were camped at Blue Nile Falls, and made a habit of robbing every Farangi who appeared. (I finally did visit Blue Nile Falls in 2015, but in the intervening 40 years a hydroelectric plant has been built which steals nearly all of the water which used to flow over the falls. The remaining falls are unimpressive, at least in November, the dry season.) Lake Tana's southeastern exit is the legendary source of the Blue Nile. I walked north from town and stood on the little bridge across the stream, only about 80 feet wide and one foot deep, and flowing gently. It was almost dreamy to realize that this water would not reach the ocean for another two thousand five hundred miles when it would finally exit the Nile Delta from Egypt into the Mediterranean. Standing above that creek brought a geographical closure to my tracing of the Nile from the Med to the source of the White Nile at Lake Victoria, and the source of the Blue, there at Lake Tana.

The next morning, I bid a none-too-fond farewell to Bahir Dar, and climbed into the luggage box of a truck headed for Gondar, to see the medieval style stone castles of that city. The Shifta had captured a petrol tanker the week before, and were said to have mined a bridge. These facts made petrol rather scarce in the mountains of Ethiopia, and had radically decreased available motor transport. The six hour trip was uneventful, but cold. I sat in the luggage box up on top of the cab, as usual, but at the early morning hour the air was extremely frigid. I had put on every stitch of clothing that I owned, and was still freezing. Have never been so cold before or since. And just to be sure that I couldn't even feel sorry for myself, the two Ethiopian passengers up there with me had their bare legs sticking out the bottom of their short shifts, and didn't seem to be bothered at all by the temperature.

## Gondar

Gondar was another dirty, flyblown town deep in the central mountains of Ethiopia, but a more interesting one. Within the town limits were three small European-medieval-style stone-and-mortar castles! Strange to see them in that part of the world. I learned that they were designed for a series of Ethiopian kings by Portuguese architects in the 1500s. They seemed rather forlorn and threadbare, each three stories tall, poorly sighted on slopes of rolling hills, within view of one another, and without any curtain walls or ditches. I toured two of them, empty and sterile inside, and viewed the smallest from the outside.

Gondar Castles

Several of the old 16th century Coptic churches on the outskirts of Gondar were visited the following morning. The ancient religious murals were really fascinating. The medieval Copts developed an artistic style uniquely their own, simple and somewhat crude, but strangely spiritual and disconnected from earthly reality. At Debre Berhan Selassie monastery, the oldest in the area, the monk/priests were pleased to see me, and showed me some amazingly beautiful illuminated parchment manuscripts written in the nearly dead ancient language of Ge'ez. Realizing that I was very interested in Ge'ez, the monks happily spoke it for me, reading responsively for several minutes. It was fascinating to actually hear the ancient tongue, kept alive by the Coptic clergy.

## Black Jews

The government bureau in Addis had informed me about the "black Jews" which were said to live in several villages not too far from Gondar. I thought it was probably just hype to encourage tourists, but decided to see what there was to be seen. My second morning in Gondar I walked several miles out of town on a dirt side road, and located Falastia, a small village not far from the track. Falastia was a farming community, being made up of about 20 round huts built of sticks and dung wattle, each about 25 feet in diameter. Most had conical thatch roofs, but a few kept out the rain with corrugated galvanized steel sheets. There were no adults to be seen at first, everyone probably being out in the surrounding fields, but the jet black kids greeted me. I did notice that each hut had a little mezuzah metal cylinder beside the door, just like every Jewish home in the US. A moment later, as I wandered around, an elderly man appeared, very black and looking like all the other Ethiopians. He displayed a ring of keys, and earnestly told me lots of things I couldn't understand. He led me to one of the huts with a sheet-metal roof, and showed me that the door was fastened by a chain and a padlock to which he had the key. I made a small contribution and we went inside. It was dark there, but in the light from the doorway I could see the altar with the star of David and the covered Torah! Kept in a wooden cupboard were some books in Hebrew. It was unmistakably a synagogue! There actually were black Jews living way back in those mountains in Ethiopia. Quite amazing. (Flash forward: Years later, in the 1980s, the Israelis paid a large fee to the Ethiopian government to be allowed to relocate those dark-skinned, isolated Jews to Israel where many still reside.) In Gondar, after three nights, I hunted around the central square seeking a truck headed north to Axum, but failed to find one. I gritted my teeth and bargained for a bus ride north.

Ethiopian Bus Stop

The loud horrible music on that bus was fully up to expectations, and as a result, I didn't enjoy the ride very much. Scenery was nothing short of spectacular, though. We traveled along the main highway north. It was built by the Italians when they were colonial overlords, and was decently maintained by the Ethiopians. All day we traveled through steep, picturesque mountains, with the road perched in a notch out of the slopes. We had mountain wall on the right side, and lots of air on the left. As I looked around this particular bus, I could see that we were getting into wilder areas. Five gentlemen passengers on the bus were carrying rifles, and two of those had bandoliers of ammunition. A funny, toothless old gent sharing a seat with me allowed me to examine his 1939 Italian-made bolt action rifle, almost certainly acquired from the Fascisti during W.W.II. He also proudly showed me his seven spare rounds of ammo, five of which actually fit his rifle.

## Shifta Ambush!

I spent most of the ride viewing the spectacular steep scenery and wishing the deafening music would stop. In the middle of the afternoon there came a sudden commotion from the front of the bus, with lots of people shouting all at once, and folks standing up, etc.. I moved to look, and saw that a big tree-trunk, maybe 18" in diameter, had been perfectly placed across the road, blocking it. We had driven into a Shifta ambush! The driver had been in this situation before, and knew exactly what to do. He never stopped, downshifted vigorously, and accelerated RIGHT ACROSS the log, one wheel at a time! The suspension screamed, and everyone was wildly tossed about inside by the four huge bumps, but we didn't hit the mountain wall on the right, nor go down the open slope on the left. Meanwhile, those with weapons had jumped to the bus windows and were firing both up and down the slope! The bus filled with the smell of rifle smoke! It was all very exciting. At the next little village we stopped, and I sifted out the story. No-one had seen any Shifta, the bus gunmen admitted that they had just been shooting to try to keep anybody's head down. Someone had been shooting back, but apparently only desultorily. There were two new bullet holes low in the body of the bus. Everyone agreed that the ambush had been set to catch a truck, and the Shifta just let the bus go on. A loaded truck would have lots more valuable stuff, and fewer defenders, and would be much, much heavier so it would be unlikely to be able to drive over the roadblock without becoming disabled. I thanked my overworked vagabond's luck that I had NOT been able to find a truck ride that particular day. If I had, I would have found myself sitting exposed up on top of the truck cab when the Shifta started shooting, and as a result, might very well not be here today to tell the tale.

After a horrible night in a stinking storeroom in Enda Selassie village, with rats running over me, screeching, and thousands of bedbugs driving me outside onto the roof in the rain, I again failed completely to find a truck ride north.

## When You Eat, I Eat

So again I punished my ears by riding an owner-operated bus. The trip was less exciting this time, flatter countryside, and with no shooting. The young man sitting behind me engaged me in English conversation. Teeling proved to be an amateur guide to the sights of Axum, and we soon made a deal. He would show me around his hometown, Axum, ancient capital of the legendary Queens of Sheba, and the only payment Teeling requested was "Every time you eat, I eat". Worked out to be a good bilateral arrangement. As I descended from the bus in Axum, my white face immediately attracted a dozen desperate-looking men, all competing for my attention. They were tourist guides, and very disappointed to find that I had already been claimed. Teeling explained to me that I was "THE tourist" in Axum for the three days I spent there. That was sobering, because Axum was Ethiopia's #1 tourist attraction. Nobody was visiting due to the many dangers, and as a result, the tourist industry there was withering. It might have also had something to do with it being the height of Ethiopia's rainy season. On my third morning in Axum I realized that I had not seen another white face for the past nine days, since I had departed Addis. That is a record for all of my vagabonding travels. There just weren't any other foreigners snooping around in the mountains of Ethiopia.

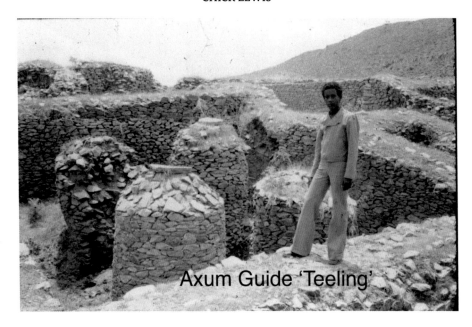

Axum Guide 'Teeling'

Teeling and I had dinner at a little hole-in-the-wall cafe in town, and talked late into the night. Next morning he reappeared, and I cooked up breakfast for us on my tiny pump-gas stove, on the floor of my cheap whorehouse room. He had never before had oatmeal! Teeling especially liked the part where we sprinkled sugar on top. We walked around together almost all day, seeing all the sights. Axum itself was quite interesting. The archaeological remains weren't much to see, and most of them were still in process of stalled excavation. It was thrilling to view the exquisite old standing stone steles scattered about. Most were thought to have been created in about 600 AD. They are thin and elegant rectangles, with some surfaces elaborately carved, ranging from 30 to 60 feet in height.

Axum was an artifact collectors paradise! The wonderful old things which were plowed up regularly by the farmers supplied half a dozen little antiquities shops in town, and those shopkeepers were really hungry for a sale. Since I was the ONLY tourist, it was a real buyers market! The coins of the Axumite civilization were very beautiful. The ancient artisans somehow figured out how to add gold inlay and/or plating to individual bronze and silver coins! I bought a thin bronze coin the size of a penny which had a small gold dot attached to the center of the Christian cross on the obverse side, and bargained for another really lovely tiny silver coin, in perfect condition, with the crown and necklace of the Axumite ruler plated with pure gold! What a wonderful piece!

## Long-Lost Ark of the Covenant

Axum also had a selection of medieval Coptic churches, including the central basilica of the entire Coptic faith. In that church was reported to reside the fabled Ark of the Covenant, the actual stone tablets carved by God and given to Moses. Yep, the same Ark which Indiana Jones raided in popular Hollywood culture. According to standard history, the Ark disappeared at the time of the Babylonian sack of Jerusalem. But the Coptic church tells a different story.

## Legend of Menelik

In biblical times, the Queen of Sheba decided to pay a visit to the wisest and most famous ruler in the world, King Solomon in Israel. She loaded up her retainers, left Axum, and sailed up the red sea, arriving in Jerusalem for a state visit. When she was presented to King Solomon, he was struck by her unusual beauty, and offered a wing of his palace to the Queen and her retinue. The Queen, wise to the ways of men, agreed conditionally upon a promise that Solomon would not try to take her into his bed. Solomon agreed to make this commitment, but only if the Queen would promise not to take anything from his palace without permission. She had no trouble agreeing to that, so the Queen and her people moved into the palace. King Solomon, however, was clever, and not to be put off easily. After the visitors had settled in, he arranged for an unusually spicy dinner to be served to the Axumites. Then, in the hall just outside the Queen's room, he placed a beaker of fresh, cold water. Late at night the Queen awakened thirsty, and went out into the hall. Finding the water she drank some, whereupon Solomon, who had concealed himself nearby, declared that since she had broken her promise by taking the water without permission, he was no longer bound by his vow. It seems that by then the Queen had developed a fondness for wise King Solomon anyway, and the state visit expanded into a conjugal one.

Months later, when the Axumites were taking their leave, it had become obvious that the Queen of Sheba was expecting. At parting, Solomon gave her a signet ring, with instructions to give it to their offspring, so that Solomon would recognize his child whenever he or she would come to Jerusalem. The Queen returned to Axum and gave birth to a boy, whom she named Menelik. When Menelik came of age, his mother informed him of his parentage, and gave him the signet ring. This was quite some news for Menelik, because King Solomon was still the most famous and powerful monarch in the world, and, since the king had not married until after the Queen of Sheba's visit, Menelik realized that he was the firstborn son of wise Solomon. He decided to travel to Jerusalem to claim his birthright. Arriving in Jerusalem with his own retainers, he presented himself and the ring to Solomon, who received him into the palace with some pomp and a fine show of affection. He made the guest wing of the palace available to Menelik and his people, and fed and clothed them. But, in the intervening years, Solomon had acquired an official wife, and by then had official offspring to whom he intended to leave the kingdom. Solomon was, in truth, not too pleased that this dark-hued bastard son had unexpectedly appeared.

After a month or so, Solomon's indifference had made it obvious to Menelik that his father did not intend to provide him with any birthright. So Menelik decided to take as his due the most sacred and valuable objects on earth, the tablets upon which God had engraved the ten commandments. Menelik had his carpenter build a box of cedar wood which was exactly the same shape and size as the Ark of the Covenant. Then his people became familiar with the guards of the Temple at Jerusalem, dropping by each night to provide stimulating drinks in the darkest hours of the boring watch. One night, after drugging the guards, Menelik stole the true Ark of the Covenant, placed his dummy box under the beautiful embroidered cloth coverings, and immediately decamped for his homeland. The Jewish Rabbis, of course, could not admit that they had lost the tablets of the covenant, and so hushed up the matter, pretending that the false box still contained the holy treasures. Menelik returned to Axum and soon was crowned Menelik I, emperor of Axum, whereupon he presented the Ark of the Covenant to the local priests. According to Coptic religious tradition, it is still there, hidden in a vault-building beside the Central basilica at Axum.

## Feast of Saint Michael

As you can imagine, I REALLY wanted to get a look at this fascinating relic, but had been told that it would be impossible. However, once in Axum, Teeling told me that the morning after I planned to depart happened to be one of the major Coptic Holidays, and as part of the ceremonies, the Patriarch planned to bring the Ark out and march it through the town in a procession! I could see it simply by staying another day. What great vagabond's luck!

On the altar of every Coptic church sits a box or carved board called a Tabot ("Tae-Bow")which is a sanctified representation the Ark of the Covenant. I asked Teeling how we could know whether we were seeing the fabled Ark itself, or only a Tabot. He said that IF the monk who had been proclaimed the Guardian of the Ark were with the box, then it would be the real thing. Those guardians serve for life, and they all reliably go blind over the years. So, on that mystical morning, deep in a remote corner of Africa, I was the only Farangi to view the amazing column of white-robed monks, interspersed with brightly colored, gloriously robed and mitered Coptic clergymen as they paced the town with a slow dignified tread. Before and after the procession strode priests swinging smoking incense censers on long chains. Horns, flutes and drums were played, and several of the party jangled clanking sistrums identical to the ones I had seen on Pharaonic bas-reliefs along the Nile !! One priest carried the holy box on his head, covered by a beautiful gold-embroidered black cloth, while two others walked beside him, sheltering it with bright parasols on poles. Teeling pointed out the blind Guardian with his milky cataracts. Since the Guardian must always be within a few feet of the genuine Ark, there was no chance it was elsewhere. I shot a whole MONTH's worth of film in a few minutes, thrilled by the exotic scene and by my good fortune. In the intervening years I have come to believe that the Feast of Saint Michael in 1975 was very likely the LAST time the actual Ark was EVER brought out of its vault. Nobody on the web seems to have newer daytime photos of it. In recent years the Tabot box joins a pre-dawn procession several times a week, but the Guardian never seems to join those processions.

The Ark of the Covenant finished its circuit through the lanes of the overgrown village of Axum, and re-entered the dark cloisters of the ancient brooding church. It was still early morning, and, already lugging my pack, I tipped Teeling generously, shook his hand, and headed to the dusty square which served Axum as a transport hub. In Addis Ababa I had been told that all travel north of Axum into the rebelling province of Eritrea was impossible due to rebel military activity which had closed the main highway. Once in Axum, I discovered that the Ethiopian army had reopened the road, and buses occasionally scooted through the war zone to the provincial capital of Asmara. My plan then changed to jumping one of those buses and subsequently finding transport from the Eritrean port of Massawa up the Red Sea to Aqaba in Jordan.

# INTO THE ERITREAN
# WAR ZONE

A deal had been brewing between one of the antiquities shopkeepers and yours truly to trade my pewter belt buckle, a heavy Ethiopian silver chain, and some cash for two more Axumite coins. I went to the shop to close the deal, but found it still closed, and the only bus headed to Asmara was about to leave. At the last possible moment when I already had one foot on the bus steps, the shopkeeper appeared, all out of breath, with the coins wrapped up in a cloth. I unwrapped them, took a glance, made a rude comment in English, turned, and boarded. The clever shyster had been watching me from hiding until he knew there was no time to check carefully, made his last-second cameo, and had tried to substitute two inferior coins for the ones we had been bargaining over. No trade. I rode the bus all day, stopping many times at army checkpoints where everyone had to get down and be searched while the soldiers searched the bus and luggage.

In the south of Ethiopia, the soldiers had been uniformly armed with old British Enfield bolt-action rifles. As I traveled North I had noted that those weapons were progressively replaced by semi-automatic M1 Garands of U.S. manufacture. There in the north of the country where the real fighting was going on, the standard weapon of the Ethiopian army was the big, heavy, almost-modern M14 rifle.

I did see two bridges which had been dynamited by the rebels.

Bulldozers had cut temporary paths around the bridges, which were being repaired. I took a good photo of a blown bridge from the bus window as we drove away. In the villages where the bus stopped I got plenty of attention from the locals. Just standing beside a tea shop, or sitting by the road on a bench I attracted crowds of dozens of people, not all begging, but standing around staring at me and speaking to one another in low voices. This was something new for me in Ethiopia. I figured it was a cultural thing, because I had encountered plenty of that behavior in Egypt, but hadn't noted it since I had reached the Sudan. Here in Eritrea perhaps the culture was more similar to Egypt. Or perhaps in that area they just hadn't ever seen many Farangi.

That morning in Axum, and while traveling to Asmara, I saw lots of children enthusiastically cracking big whips! I saw others pounding big fleshy succulent-plant leaves between rocks to get at the strong internal fibers which they braided to make their bullwhips. Whips were in some curious way related to the particular Coptic Holy Day, the Feast of St. Michael, and cracking the whips was a traditional way to make celebratory music. Strange customs in Ethiopia.

## Pre-Owned Protective Charms

At one of those untrammeled village stops I found a street vendor sitting beside the road on a blanket upon which he had spread his wares. He had nothing but used junk, but the stuff included two little amulets for sale. Almost every Ethiopian and Eritrean wore a little flat, square leather pouch on a thong around his neck. I had heard that there were protective magical charms inside each one, and I was interested to learn more about them. I decided to buy one to disassemble, and another one to keep intact. So I began to bargain for his two little protective amulets, which had obviously spent many years at someone's throat. This attracted a pretty good crowd of interested spectators. We finally reached agreement, I paid the man, and he handed over the charms. I immediately pulled out my pocketknife and slit open the side of one amulet. Instant PANDEMONIUM! The vendor LEAPED to his feet and backed away fast, shouting something! Everyone else hollered and squawked and moved smartly away from me! Just from the tone and facial expressions I know that the message pounding me from all sides was **"WHY the HELL did you do THAT!?!?!?!"** In a heartbeat I went from the middle of a claustrophobic crowd of passive onlookers to a lone figure in the center of a ring of suspicious, gesticulating, startled people with nobody closer than 40 feet! I slowly closed the knife and put it and both amulets into my pocket. This response calmed the scene down considerably. I still don't know exactly what felony I had committed by cutting open the charm packet, but I have a theory. Perhaps the little charms absorb the bad things from which they protect the wearers, and perhaps I had released all of that evil. I usually am not that stupid and culturally unaware. That evening, in the privacy of my cathouse room, I checked out my acquisition. Inside the little flat leather envelope was a very thin sheet of oiled, scraped animal skin, all slick and greasy. This sheet had been carefully inscribed with lots of Ethiopian writings, various mystical signs, and lots of magic number squares using Arabic, Roman, and unknown numerals. The sheet was about 8" square, and had been elaborately folded in a strange helical/accordion pattern to fit into the 1" square amulet package. What a treasure! That experience triggered in me an interest in magic number squares which lasted until I found myself laid up badly injured in a Bosnian hospital with time on my hands (but that is another story). There I worked out for myself a system to create magic number squares of almost any dimension, and summing to any desired number, at which point their cachet of mystery evaporated.

## *Asmara*

We arrived in Asmara the following morning. Though well inland, that city had a much more Mediterranean feel to it, with western alphabet signs, the occasional Italian restaurant, and even a gelati shop. I did see other white folks, mostly Italian looking young gents with natty clothes and slick hairstyles. Everywhere I went in Asmara, the kids immediately shouted "Americani!" I know that I am indistinguishable from a German or a Dutchman to the eye, so it was something of a mystery how they always had me correctly pegged as American.

Walking down a street with my pack on, searching for cheap lodging, I heard a sudden commotion behind me, and spun around, ready for anything! Two small Eritrean men had BURST out of their office just after I passed! They were grinning widely, speaking English to me, and excitedly almost picked me up to carry me back into their little travel agency! The travel agents served me good sweet hot tea, and explained that they were so happy to see me because I was the first overland tourist they had seen in about eight months. Their business had really been hurting! I figured this was a substantial exaggeration, just setting me up so I would buy an air ticket from them. I told them my plans to travel north on the Red Sea, and they told me about a wonderful airfare they could offer me to Athens, via Addis Ababa, Khartoum, and Cairo. With the help of the travel agents I located a nearby house of prostitution, signed in, and took a room. I had the usual hassle with the pretty professional girls, two of whom knocked at my door, invited themselves in to visit, wore out their few words of English, and then sat in my room forever, intently watching everything I did. I finally couldn't stand the sexual tension and scrutiny anymore, and gently ejected them. I guess I'm just not a very good host.

Asmara at the time was a very tense place. Police and soldiers were everywhere. There was an 8 PM to 5AM curfew, and the story was that the army really did shoot you without warning if you were out and about. The streets were patrolled even in daytime by big open military trucks full of soldiers with machine guns mounted on the tops of the cabs. The soldiers looked scared and jumpy, which is a really bad sign. I heard automatic weapon fire in the streets every night but one. I never did find any empty AK-47 cartridges on the streets in the daytime, though I looked for them.

## *Kagnew Station*

I ate some Gelati, but it just didn't quite hit the spot. It had been more than six months since I'd had any American ice cream. My travel agent buddies had told me about an American Navy communications base on the outskirts of Asmara called Kagnew Station. I took a horse cab out to the American base and spent half an hour trying to talk my way past the Eritrean-manned guard post at the gate of the huge, fenced compound. The guards weren't buying any of my fast talk, and were ignoring my American passport, though they were glad enough to smoke my cigarettes.

Then a big, flashy Chrysler pulled up to the gate behind me, driven by a white guy sporting granny glasses with red lenses, a bright colored paisley shirt, and a huge blond afro hairdo. "What's goin' on here, Herbert?" He asked. The ranking guard reported deferentially, and handed the freak behind the wheel my passport. He looked it over, glanced at me, and said, "S' ok, let him in", then drove onto the base. When asked, Herbert informed me that the flaky-looking guy was John Morris, the civilian head of Kagnew Station security!

I found my way to the PX and cafeteria, empty at that time of day. The subsidized prices were so low as to be negligible, and the Eritrean kitchen staff of 5 people fixed me up a chili dog, fried onion rings, and a big bowl of vanilla ice cream, which I really enjoyed. I followed that up with another chili dog, onion rings, and ice cream. While I was eating, the security head and another freaky-looking white guy came into the cafeteria with two of the most beautiful women I have ever seen in my life. All four of them sat at another table. Those Eritrean ladies were really stunning, high cheekbones, almond eyes, young, slender, perfectly coiffed and made up, wearing long, slinky, expensively designed and custom-tailored low-cut gowns. They were speaking lovely, American-accented English, and speaking it well. I hadn't seen anything like them for quite a long time. And it was still the morning!

When my repast was finished, I wandered over to their table to thank Morris for allowing me to visit the PX. We did mutual introductions, and they asked where I had flown in from, and why. When I admitted that I had been come in from Axum the day before, four jaws went slack with surprise. "There haven't been any Farangi up that road for over six months!" exclaimed John. "How did you avoid the army checkpoints?" When I revealed that I had been passed through by at least six checkpoints, their amazement increased. "Every foreigner that tried that route lately was stopped at the first checkpoint, arrested, and escorted clean back to Addis, five days hard travel, for very unfriendly interrogation!" The only explanation that makes any sense to me is that, since I came through the war zone on the Feast of St. Michael, the "big fish" soldiers must have all taken the day off, and the "little fish" that were left wouldn't take responsibility to seize me and send me back, so I slipped through. Just chalk it up to strong vagabond's luck.

After confirming me as the only foreigner to pass through the Eritrean war zone in 6 months, the head of Kagnew Station security said, "Too bad you didn't get any photos of the blown bridges, they're worth $500 each to the news services." I grabbed the heavy leather belt pouch containing my little camera and admitted that I had taken a good photo. "Well, take the film out of your camera right now", said John. "It won't be long until the Ethiopians realize what happened." So I took out the almost finished roll of film and put it in my skivvies, replacing it with the spare roll in my pouch. John offered to let me use the base postal service to send the film out of the country, because the Ethiopians didn't interfere with Kagnew Station mail. Back at my room in town I packed up that film, with all of my treasures and gifts for my family. Into 2 boxes went strings of ostrich egg beads, my lovely ancient Axumite coins, my magical protective charms, everything that I had been lugging around with me that wasn't necessary to keep on traveling.

All Chick's
African Jewelry

I went back onto the base early the next afternoon for a party to which John had invited me, and handed over the packages with my film. I gave Mr. Morris money for the postage, and looked around at the other Americans. It immediately became obvious why all the kids in Asmara always called me "Americani". Of the dozen white civilians partying, 10 of them were longhaired hippie-looking types! Since no white locals of Italian extraction would be caught DEAD with long hair, my long tresses had marked me as another American in their eyes.

# Local Girlfriends

And a few more things were learned at that party. Kagnew Station in 1975 was only a shadow of what it had been previously. From 5000 Americans at its height, the whole station now was only 14 swabbies and 30 American civilians. At the party were 12 American males, mostly technical types, as well as 14 of the really stunningly attractive Eritrean females I spoke of earlier. Each of the Americans had a classy local girlfriend, whose sole job in life was to look really good for him, and keep his brasswork highly polished! The spare pair of women were the girlfriends of Americans who had recently bugged out, due to the danger and the war and the rockets which occasionally dropped onto the base. Those two gals still had their base passes. The reason all of those "girlfriends" were so terrifyingly attractive is that they were the survivors. You see, there were originally a couple of thousand of these girlfriends, and as Americans would leave, the finest ladies left behind would be picked up by the remaining guys, who would trade in their previous, less desirable girlfriends. Needless to say, the two dozen who had "made the cuts" were really something, and the competition between these women in clothes, hair and sex-appeal was vicious!

Managing to get back to my lodging before curfew, surely enough, there were two Ethiopian military policemen waiting for me, one of whom spoke good English. They knew where I had been, because I had signed the hotel check-in papers honestly, and they demanded my camera. I argued with them successfully, so they only took my film. I rewound the film much longer than necessary to make them believe it was not a new roll, and handed it over. They immediately broke open the tough little yellow canister, exposing the film to the light. After I signed a confusing document, mostly in Amharic, in which I committed, among other things, to not go back through the war zone or suffer serious penalties, they departed satisfied. That night I heard two small explosions in town, but for once didn't hear any of the characteristic "popping" sounds made by an AK47.

## Eritrean Liberation Front
## Hits the base

When I dropped into the base the following day, things had changed dramatically, and everyone was milling about looking concerned. The Eritrean Liberation Front had cut through the perimeter wire onto a remote part of the base during the night and kidnapped two American and four Eritrean radio technicians! They had also stolen a big yellow all-terrain vehicle. Those kidnapped were Steve Campbell and Jim Harrel, two guys I had partied with only a few hours before the abduction. The ELF obviously had very good intelligence, because that night was the one time when both of the best American radio technicians, at shift change, were together at that exposed post. Everyone knew that the ELF radio had been off-line for about a week. The Kagnew Americans weren't too worried about their friends, because they figured the ELF had taken them to fix the radio, and would release them as soon as they had completed their task. This was the pattern which had been followed the last time Americans were kidnapped by the freedom fighters.

## Job Offer

Even so, this new development caused four of the few remaining American civilians to toss it in and leave Eritrea. Since I had admitted my Uni degree in Physics, and was perfectly comfortable with electronic equipment, these defections resulted in an immediate offer of a lucrative technical job at the base. I must admit that I considered it, but for all of the wrong reasons. When my suspect motives became clear to me, I declined. The major attraction, I realized, would have been "auditioning" the six newly-unattached girlfriends, several of whom were already circling me in predatory fashion, showing me subtle little marks of affection, like putting their arms around me from behind, or sitting facing me astride my knee. Reality for the abducted pair turned out to be quite bleak. My parents followed the story and kept me informed by letter. Those two Americans were held captive for the next 18 months, before finally being released unharmed. So, the ELF broke into a gated US military compound to get two US hostages, and there I was, happily motoring through the war zone on a bus! Seems it might have been much easier to grab me.

My fifth morning in Asmara I hopped a bus along the beautiful 65 mile route down from the highlands to the grotty port of Massawa, including my first views of the Red Sea. I spent five hours at the docks, frustrated by failing to find any sea transport headed for Aqaba. Hard information was extremely difficult to come by. I took the bus back to Asmara in the late afternoon, beating sunset by a full hour.

Since I couldn't leave by road, nor apparently by sea, I deciding to take the cheap flight to Athens. I changed money on the black market, incidentally defusing two different attempts to cheat me. The flight was about 3000 miles all told, for $107. If I had changed money in a bank, the price would have been $153.

## *Return to Cairo*

Layover was long enough in Addis that I managed to dash into town from the airport and pick up some precious mail waiting forlornly in Poste Restante!   Mail from home was always a huge treat. After bouncing at the airport in Khartoum, I arrived at Cairo airport at about midnight. I discovered three inexperienced French gents standing timidly together back to back in the terminal, all with brand-new, shining backpacks, fresh from Paris. A pack of predatory Egyptian hustlers and confidence men were clustered all around them. When I approached them in a friendly fashion, and greeted them in bad but understandable French, they took a look at the mud of Eritrea still on my boots and attached themselves desperately to me. I got them outside, and bargained for a cheap taxi, split four ways, for the 40 mile, dark drive into central Cairo.

## Taxi Shakedown

Halfway there, in the middle of nowhere, and a very dark part of the road, the taxi driver pulled over to the side. He then explained that he wanted half of the fare now, and that his version of half was twice the total bargained-for price. He claimed that the agreed fare was "each" which meant we owed him four times as much. Since those unfamiliar with Egypt might fear to be dropped off in the middle of dark nowhere, it should have been a pretty good scam. As proof of this, when I explained what was going on to the Frenchmen, they were eager to pay the ripoff, being terrified of being dropped off way out there, and I had to shout at them to get them to shut up. I then calmly climbed out of the front seat and started to pull my backpack from the luggage rack. The Frenchmen whimpered and whined, and I had to holler at them again to get them out of the taxi. Finally the driver understood that I was perfectly willing to get down there in the dark, that he wasn't getting a piaster until the agreed ride was completed, and that the proper fare was all he could hope for. Soon we arrived in central Cairo. The driver's perfidy cost him his otherwise substantial tip.

Now at about 2 am, I marched us to all seven cheap hotels with which I was familiar before we gave up. Every inexpensive bed in Cairo was booked that night. I led my new French friends to the gardens of the snooty Nile Hilton, to try to hide well enough to get some sleep. Nope, a uniformed guard spotted us and came over to eject us. I used my rusty Arabic on him, and gave away some cigarettes, and he was so impressed that he showed us the best place to sleep, deep in the rose garden, and promised to watch over us, and to get the guy on the next shift to do the same. The inexperienced French travelers then concluded that I was a minor vagabonding god. So, we got a few hours of much needed sleep, awakening and stretching the next morning in full view of a hundred expensive hotel windows above.

And what became of my photos of rebel-dynamited bridges? Of course, John Morris stole them from me, either to sell, or for his American Intelligence community bosses, and had to steal all of my other things as well so that he could claim they were lost by the US Postal Service. I never saw the boxes again, nor any of the wonderful things inside. I really regret losing all the photos, including those of the Ark of the Covenant. Somehow I have always felt that Mr. Morris and I will meet up again someday for a little reckoning. If so, that day is still in the future. (Please be sure to continue reading through the added chapter.)

## *Out of Africa*

All in all, it had been exactly 99 days from the time I left Egypt into Darkest Africa until the time I returned. Even though my vagabond's world tour stretched to more than 1200 days, those were probably the most interesting 99 consecutive days of my life. At least those have proved to be the most interesting 99 days so far. Yeah, I can dream.

I have quite enjoyed re-reading my 1975 daily journals and letters home. Writing up the tales really brought the past back with a surprising immediacy.

# NEW CHAPTER ADDED 4 YEARS LATER IN 2003

For those interested in these vagabonding stories, I have added a chapter to my trek through Africa. It primarily concerns the treasure boxes sent to California from Eritrea which never arrived. I really missed those photos of the Ark of the Covenant, because whenever I told the story of seeing it, my listeners would be rapt until I claimed my film was stolen by a government agent. This blatant bit of conspiracy theory always ripped the bottom out of my personal credibility, and the listeners eyes invariably clouded with suspicious disbelief. As a result, I stopped recounting the tale of having actually seen the Ark.

## Curious E-mail

I received an interesting email in February '03. The subject line asked "Ever hear the sound of Ge'ez?" This climbed well above the level of lowest-common-denominator spam. The sender "JAMOR", who had read this account on the Miskatonic University website, claimed to be that selfsame John Morris who had appropriated my stuff so long ago, and, strangely, he didn't seem to be pissed off that I had labeled him a thief in a public forum. Responding cautiously, I learned that JAMOR was living near San Francisco, and claimed to have been seeking me, because, unbelievably, he still had my lost treasure boxes after all those 28 years! As you can imagine, this news excited me greatly. After some time to reflect, however, I realized that "JAMOR" was actually a predatory web-troll who discovered the story and decided to manipulate my desires and con me into disgorging money. That explanation fit the data perfectly. I was very disappointed but decided that there was no reason not to play out the hand I had been dealt. I continued an occasional exchange of emails with the purported Mr. Morris pretending to still believe he was genuine. Some detailed questions about Kagnew station were asked, and he responded promptly with very plausible information. I did a web search for Kagnew and immediately found a website with pretty much the same answers in pretty much the same wording he had used in the answer. Soon I was told that JAMOR had been out of work for a long time, and that his vehicle had a broken water pump which he could not afford to repair. Yep, it all fit. Soon funds would be requested to enable something or other. Continued pretending to be deceived by this confidence scam.

On a Sunday evening in March I found email from "JAMOR" stating "I got your stuff from my storage unit today and I'll send it on to you." That was unexpectedly direct, and the message included an attachment. As the jpeg opened, the image came up slowly through my dial-up connection, raster-ing from the top and continuing with incrementally increasing detail. I clutched the arms of my chair in amazement! The screen was forming a digital photo of the contents of my African Treasure Boxes, packed up 28 years previously, and lost for all those years! The photo had been labeled by JAMOR, (who now without doubt WAS John Morris, himself), with little arrows pointing to "geodes" and "Ektachrome 64 : 36 exposure". Yes, the digital image showed a silver film can. And just to remove any possible doubt, smiling out at me from the image was a 1975 visa photo of myself! Yowee, - - - could have knocked me onto my back with a feather!

So, HOW could he possibly still have my stuff? The actual cloak-and-dagger tale is WAY better than any I could have invented. John explained that as I left Asmara (after the kidnapping of the American radio techs), the Ethiopians began to intercept the Kagnew station mail. John decided that he would hold my boxes until things calmed down. Then, probably, he forgot about my stuff, understandable with everything else he had going on as head of base security in a war zone. A year and a half later, the US-allied Ethiopian artillery started firing into Kagnew Station, and everything in Asmara went to hell for the handful of Americans remaining. John himself had to bug out of Eritrea with only two hours notice! He had barely enough time to phone his local agents, telling them "Hide my stuff!", flying out on the next-to-last flight evacuating the base. His local people packed up and buried John's papers, journals and other things, but subsequently LOST CONTROL of the hiding place, and could not get back to the site to retrieve them! This uncomfortable situation maintained itself for 23 years!! Finally, what John described as a "window of opportunity" opened, and the still-faithful local agents, in a stealthy midnight operation, returned to the cache, unearthed it, and shipped the stuff to John in San Francisco, probably at great personal risk and considerable expense. (I know more about this than I am permitted to tell you, to protect the faithful locals.) John was, I'm sure, surprised to discover that my treasure boxes had all along accompanied his own things in hiding, although my name and the "mail to" address had been lost. He began an abiding, casual search for that now-nameless vagabond, intending, if possible, to get my things back into my hands. On that day in February, running a web search for his own name and Kagnew Station, John discovered my travelogue on the (defunct after 2011) Miskatonic University website. Mr. Morris generously shipped me the contents of those boxes at his own expense!

When I had them in my hands I arranged an opening celebration at my parents' house, to which they had been addressed so long ago. The boxes were opened and the original notes inside were read out loud. (I was quite relieved that my 1975 notes did not sound as though they were written by a complete jerk.)

As you might imagine, this was an exceedingly strange and wonderful occasion! All of my treasures were there, including the ostrich eggshell beads, the Axumite coin, and a fired clay frog (made by the black Jews) sent as what the notes termed my Mother's "belated birthday present". What a thrill! Also demonstrated was the shaky reliability of unaided memory. The box notes made clear that there had only ever been one roll of developed film, and one ancient Axumite coin, in spite of my memories which included more of each. To repay John Morris for his kindness, I contracted with a buddy to hand-paint seven detailed miniature figures representing Eritrean traditional warriors, since I knew that JAMOR admired those guys. When John received them, he sent me back a photo of the miniature fighters guarding his Lava Lamp.

# Fate of the Film

Now there remained to discover if any images might still be on the undeveloped roll of color slide film, in spite of all that it had suffered. I searched the world for specialist film-development labs and found several (Italy, Canada) which could develop the film, but only in black and white, as the chemical solutions needed to process Ektachrome were no longer manufactured. That didn't sound good to me, so the search continued for weeks until a lab in Colorado claimed they would color develop the abused antique film. Rocky Mountain Photo Labs collected undeveloped Ektachrome from customers worldwide until they had enough to make it worth their while to hand-mix a batch of the proper development solutions ! They warned me, however, that I had to pay in advance, that it would be very expensive, that it might be six months before development occurred, and that, although Ektachrome has a reputation for being the most stable film ever produced, it was quite unlikely that any recoverable images would still be on the film. The exorbitant advance payment demanded was only $24! The precious roll headed for Colorado pronto!

Developed slides reappeared in five weeks, and while the colors have faded badly, the images are there !   I am once again permitted to see the children at Marsabit displaying their little jack-o-lanterns, the rebel-dynamited bridge, and the Ark of the Covenant being carried on its circuit through Axum ! Big prints and cropped blowups of the best Ark photos were created by a custom lab in Hollywood, and they came out rather well.

This is, of course, impossible.

It can be very accurately calculated to have zero probability.

There is NO WAY on this familiar planet that I should be able to see these long-lost photographs, after twenty-eight years.

That I do, in truth, hold them in my hands, has badly shaken my comfortable faith in the laws of probability and basic physics. I am not complaining. I will happily adjust to this strange new universe where absolutely impossible things DO occasionally happen.

(See below for the images recovered after 28 years !)

Rebel-Dynamited Bridge

Recovered after 28 years

(photo recovered after 28 years, more below)

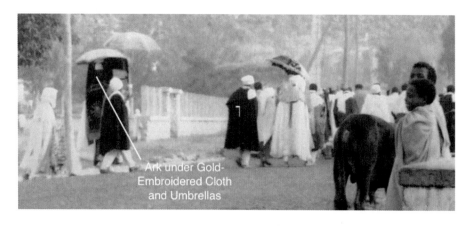

Ark under Gold-
Embroidered Cloth
and Umbrellas

Distant Ark
with Cow Butts

Image
Recovered
after 28
years, more
below

Distant Ark
Blow-Up

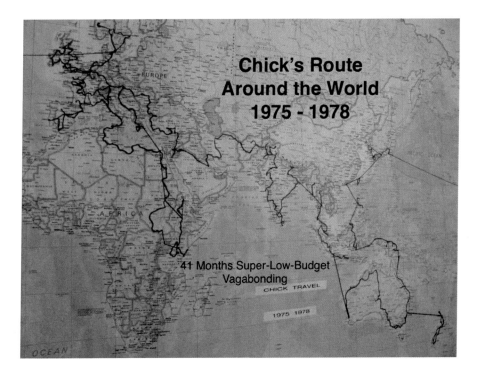

Chick's Route
Around the World
1975 - 1978

41 Months Super-Low-Budget
Vagabonding
CHICK TRAVEL
1975 1978

Made in the USA
Middletown, DE
14 July 2023